MW01147963

SOUL AND SUBSTANCE

Soul and Substance

A Poet's Examination Papers

Jay Wright

PRINCETON UNIVERSITY PRESS
PRINCETON AND OXFORD

Published by Princeton University Press
41 William Street, Princeton, New Jersey 08540
99 Banbury Road, Oxford OX2 6JX

press.princeton.edu

All Rights Reserved

ISBN 9780691245959
ISBN (pbk.) 9780691245966
ISBN (e-book) 9780691246024

British Library Cataloging-in-Publication Data is available

Editorial: Anne Savarese and James Collier
Production Editorial: Mark Bellis
Text and Cover Design: Heather Hansen
Production: Lauren Reese
Publicity: Jodi Price and Carmen Jimenez
Copyeditor: Daniel Simon

This book has been composed in Arno Pro

10 9 8 7 6 5 4 3 2 1

CONTENTS

On Death: A Speculative
Approach to Death's Future

Consider now a man and his wife in a New England village, where the only things available to them are the various sets of relationships that the village makes possible. One learns the proximity and ubiquity of death. I should have said the man and the woman learn these things, or they learn a fundamental instance of a phenomenon called death. Why walk around this word? Why not acknowledge that this text relies upon a fundamental insistence that would make no sense to the movement begun through a questioning that never finds its center apart from an implied absence? That point throws us into contradiction.

Can a book be about death? Can we find a grounding for an experience that is beyond us? Can we make that experience speak in revelatory fashion about contingent experiences? It would seem that introducing that impulse, as I have called it, would do away with the necessity in experiential exploration, make us sit fascinated by an operation we can neither initiate nor control.

What does it mean to initiate death? We sit with a particular provocation. We cannot simply mean that we cannot bring death about, our own or that of another human, or that of any material being, or that of any substantial or insubstantial complex. There, at the end, we have an evasion. We scoot around the suggestion of being by suggesting an epistemological complexity. For we know that, in speaking of these various forms of possible deaths, we cannot say what constitutes death in each case. And we cannot proceed as though death in one domain meant the same thing in the next domain, or even had the same meaning on a subsequent occurrence that obtained on a previous occurrence within the same domain. Put it simply. Can the old guy dying in the green house at the head of the street be treated intellectually or emotionally as we would treat with

3

the middle-aged woman who expired in the white house next to his? What shall we say, to continue in perplexity, of the porcupines I dispatched in Hamilton's barn? What manner of deaths are these?

If we think at all about this matter, we have to acknowledge that we cannot mean the same emotional and intellectual engagement in every death we encounter. That becomes apparent at its most trivial level when we think of individual deaths. We respond at a different depth to the death of someone with whom we have been familiar, talked with, lived with, perhaps loved. We need not go to any extraordinary level of intimacy to find that we are moved by a particular death.

Why should this be so? I think the answer, or a part of the answer, lies in the imaginative weight we bring to bear on a particular death. Put crudely, at this point, death engages our imagination, and the imagination becomes a function in the process of a particular death. We have, at that moment, learned to escape abstraction and obscurity through an imaginative realization of a singular moment. This death we confront at this moment cannot be any other death we have encountered; we fall out of our conceptual habit. We cannot in this case appeal to conceptualization. I almost said to memory. You might think that you could call upon memory. Calling upon memory might seem an appeal to experience. Certainly, even the innocent can appeal to experience; certainly, even those with a small fund of experience have imagination. And we almost have to argue that that escape from abstraction and obscurity relies upon an imaginative apprehension that one acquires without effort.

That last assertion makes us uneasy. Imagination cannot come without effort. Nor can we simply dispense with the obscurity that surrounds any particular death. We work very hard to avoid a definition, specifying the properties of death, doing away with that salutary obscurity that surrounds us. It would seem that we hold onto the obscurity because it makes imagination possible; we can speak, almost as though we had become theologians, of justification. That has a nice bell to it: the justified imagination.

What does it mean? How are we to effect passage into other domains where other forms of death reside? We have to move toward understanding, toward a myriad of forms of understanding what constitutes vitality—long before we ever come to terms with death. Classicists have sought to instruct us about the necessary preparation for life's ending. We find these essays comforting, say, at most, but we are left with a nagging sense of ineptitude, of misapprehension, misconception and inadequacy. I have spent some recent time burrowing among the biologists. Population is on my mind, the uniqueness of everything in the organic world. A classicist becomes much too essentialist for this turbulent mind. Now, who's at fault—the classicist, or the one who has set himself the task of making sense of the variability and creative depth of death? So the question might not be how does one prepare for death, or even how does one live, or prepare the dignity of a specific departure. The question rises to face us again. What do we do when we die? When can we say that we have accomplished our death? When does that transformation of consciousness occur? And of what are we conscious?

We get into trouble here because we think we have to admit that consciousness is just about all that we have of death. But consciousness of that singular event appears to be just what we do not have. We might find it absurd to say that we cannot see or recognize a lifeless body. The porcupine I have just hammered with my twelve-gauge is most dead. The hollow tree that no longer puts forth its leaves has died. My father, lying in his casket, has expired. We have thorough evidence of life's with-drawal wherever we turn; we have countless ways of expressing this recognition. What we recognize is the cessation of a pro-cess. Yet there we have another problem. Can we speak of death, too, as a process? When can we say that that process has ceased? Need we say that the process has stopped? Is this all that we can mean by the consciousness of death?

I find myself becoming too ingenious with regard to the complexity that a certain form of experience asks, and threaten to become a ventriloquist, a magician adept at divining the physical language of objects and other forms of being. No mea-sure of experience can ever give me insight into the develop-mental contingency of a wren or a white-tailed deer. Nothing will inform me of a possible sentience and consciousness in an uprooted oak. Have we created a functional or an interpretive problem for ourselves by this pretense of applying a singularly inexact term to the whole of existence? My terminological in-genuity is a heritage I should refuse.

Metaphor entices us. Indirection appeals. I can, and per-haps feel I must, speak of "a certain form of experience," as though the many forms of existence could remain, or would re-main, within the same natural bounds and follow always and everywhere the same configurational movement and intent. We beg the question of natural bounds, overlooking that we have no license to think of any configurational movement as natural.

The deepest sorrow makes us impatient with subtleties and contingencies. We seem almost incapable of attending to what distinguishes one form of existence from another. What provokes this urge to tie these words, experience and existence? I almost had an answer to a question I had not intended to ask, by approaching that sorrow that defines, that event that appears common to all existence. I have to step away for a moment.

Years ago, l lived the roughshod life of a young man in voluntary exile in Mexico. I learned there to resist my inertia; I knew myself alive. I found myself clothed with an existence that sheltered me against that particular "form of existence," though death, in its every manifestation, was all around me. I lived beyond death, or, as Berta Zapata would have it, más intensamente. At this distance, I seem to have lived closer to death. Certainly, anyone who had the nerve to associate with the stranger, meaning with me, displayed a high tolerance for risk, and for improvisation, for making do, for the delights of social ambiguity. One so endowed would find some pertinent fancy in death, and be willing to play in the gifted urbanity of graveyards. One learns to speak respectfully of that urbanity, if only to avoid an intimation of the primitive. Is it the case that my Mexico harbored the ancient insanities we attribute to the primitive mind? Can we account for this intensity we experience by referring to the evasions of such a febrile mind? Wouldn't it be better to see the Mexicans' playful encounter with death as the first step, or perhaps an iterative step, toward a historical conceptualization, the evidence of a process that leads to an altered consciousness? I could, for example, return to my beginning in this interlude, and treat certain terms as defining a domain as specific as any scientific or theological domain—words that would serve this structured domain with the intensity of an unimpeachable logic, while they simultaneously restructured other domains in which these words are found. Think of "inertia," "the form of existence," and the resonance in "clothed" and "sheltered." In a sense, nothing I had done in Mexico, no report of my activity I could make, could be anything but a transposition of terms and an opening onto a new field. El día de los muertos is not my day of the dead, even if I speak the language.

I am rushing from commonality, and doing so seems an offense to common sense. Do we need an ostensive definition of death? Do we need a statistical account of its appearance throughout phenomenological existence? We point, but we have no real assurance of the phenomenon to which we point, and it is possible to believe that, however defined, that phenomenon is not ubiquitous, does not hold its shape even in those places where it does appear.

What does hold its shape in this regard? The question has paralyzed me for days. I should wonder how to go on, how to approach an inevitable confrontation without giving in to sentimentality or redundancy. These latter terms have to set bounds we thought we had transcended. We began a page threatening to do away with common measures, with sensible impulses that would tie us to that sentimentality and redundancy that can only obscure whatever makes a particular death of any interest or of any significance. And here we have come to an impasse over form—the form of a particular event; we must say the shaping of a particular event, or at least one that offers itself as a possible, if not the most productive, maneuver.

So, where have we come, if we now muck about with defensive maneuvers? If I concentrate upon brushing aside any impulses that resemble or that might in fact be impulses from the past, how does the intuition accomplish its work? It has to strike us that every gesture we might have made induces our intuition, an imaginative flowing toward a physical and psychic solution to a problem that insists upon its consequentiality. Perhaps I could close the problem by simply removing it from a necessary consideration to one that binds us to no solution. You might look upon this as a coward's way out. Such a move reminds me of my annoyance with that Berkeley colloquium that taught me the difference between subsistence and existence.

What frame can I now erect to begin the construction of an attitude toward death? But wouldn't that be the most egregious evasion? Think of the bad faith that turns the contemplation of death into a logical demonstration. I ask myself whether this inquiry wants its roots in logic. What kind of logic could at all be adequate to embody such a demonstration? I have proposed, most trivially, the idea that we often satisfy ourselves with an attitude toward death, a stance, a position, an appropriate behavior.

Isn't this a hell of a way to talk about death? As though some fidgety critic had determined that our primary task remains appropriate behavior, and has insisted that all that really matters lies in our abilities to subject the fact of death to rules by which we, and we alone, can determine its weight and consequence. This weight and this consequence will depend upon whatever contingencies in our social lives guide us at that moment. I have introduced the word—once again—contingency. Someone will rightfully say there is nothing at all contingent about death. You, yourself, someone will shout, have spoken of inevitability.

Cast the word aside, this contingency. If it must pass here, some will say, the word has to be more appropriately applied to life. What more contingent than life? The most astringent among us, if not to say the most adventurous among us, might give us that astringent tautology, life is contingency. What animates our quarrel with such an equation? Perhaps we begin in error, trying to extract a pattern of eventful behavior that would mark that behavior as life. We want to submit to an inescapable logic, one that will lead to the closure we call death. We have arrived at a difficult pass here. Questions overwhelm us. What would be the value of logic if we had to submit each individual death to the same investigation, as though the properties of each were uniformly given. There I go, off on a tangent, racing dizzily away from the seeming logic of this argument. But how can it be apparent that an individual death has only those properties that are common to all deaths? You will quarrel with me now over the absurdity of speaking of the properties of an individual death, as though we needed a designation of properties to sustain our engagement with the fact of death. You will tax me with the difficulty of uncovering those attributes that an individual death displays. Can we speak of contingency as an attribute of life? Have we determined that contingency is not an attribute of death? Cast that word, contingency, aside.

But I haven't finished with the knot at the heart of this particular phenomenon. A surly Brobdingnag had raised its head for a moment. We wanted to acknowledge closure as a phenomenological event. That's a sentence, almost, again, an evasion. We pretend that all things come to an end. Experience teaches that. We can get into a new fix by investigating experience, or more exactly, investigating its many forms. There are those among us capable of plausibly arguing for and representing the experience of a Sonoran mud turtle (and I do not mean the poet with a presumptive imagination). So perhaps we can say that these same cognoscenti could plausibly give us the sense of defining closure from the turtle's point of view. Oh, don't be absurd, you say, forget this anthropomorphizing. That is precisely what I want to do, and precisely the reason I am finding it so difficult to be exact, to say anything incontestable about death.

We have rounded on ourselves. We skirted into a consideration of life, believing that, by doing so, we would open a path to the understanding of death. We have only moved from one insecurity to another. Why should this be so? Why can't we take death as a definitive end, the final mark upon existence?

The answer lies in the assertion that there are many forms of existence.

Does that take genius? Forgive me. The commonplace benignity of that paragraph's last sentence brings me close to my own closure, that is to say, brings me close to silence. And it is the silence to which one has to appeal, not as substrate but as substance. I have, I am sure, too often referred to a notion, gleaned from ill-remembered and poorly interpreted classical Chinese texts, that proposes silence as structure. The pilgrim at work on this text would very much like to yoke these disparate notions that have surfaced here, to see closure as a dominant element of structure and to see silence shading into the substantial domain that closure commands. Could we then turn to address that final mark upon existence? Could we have, by a roundabout route, given substance to existence, and have made it possible to measure the dimension of death? But, wait, we have a problem. We seem to have introduced the question we had been able to avoid. If it is permissible to speak of the many forms of existence, isn't it conceivable to speak of the many dimensions of death? You find nothing logical in this; you accuse the pilgrim of proposing death's dimensions as a tactical maneuver. I have no defense; I cannot appeal to logic; I can only apologetically appeal to intuition. We seem to be on the road to surfeit. Anyone set against an investigation of this sort will argue that terms multiply here without a trace of utility. Singular terms propagate along an ill-defined linear progression and turn up miraculously inscribed with a multiplicity of attributes, with uncharted dimensions and connections to supposedly unrelated terms. We are, it must be said, really at work upon relation.

You might sit in a dark room, in a meditative attitude, with the morning light gradually erasing the shadows. You might see few, or none, of the objects in the room, but unless the room has nothing in it other than you and the chair, your body enters into definable relationships with everything in the room. I want to borrow a notion I have only recently encountered, and speak of the judgment embodied in aesthetic perception—that is, of the idea that such perception admits of degrees. Can we manage the outrageous notion that the body upon that chair enjoys variable relationships (I want to call it relationships of varying degree) with the many objects in the room, even with the room itself? I do not mean anything as simple as an individual preference for or a delight in any particular object or group of objects, though it is safe to imagine that, even in the dark, the impress (call it memory) of some particular object or grouping remains stronger than others. Something happens to us while we take notice of the room, its contents, its relationships, the configuration of particular rhythms. For it is the evolution of particular rhythms that we notice in taking notice. We give—I almost said, we make—the dynamics of the room's relationships; we establish the rhythms by which we know that we are there in the room. There, I have errored in implicating everyone in this room's structure. To be rigorous, I should speak only of the singular. We cannot get our minds around the abstraction of a collective body on a chair.

In just such fashion we cannot approach the idea of death's dimensions without awakening to its many degrees of relations. I risk saying that we can—not to say, we must—find analogy in the notion of death's dimensions and a many-valued degree of life's relationships.

I work to avoid slipping in an analogical bog. I cannot mean to say that any particular life will round to an inevitable and very particular death. Should we think of the oak outside the window, and watch its leaves fray and its bark go wormy, and reason that the accident of arboreal life will someday seize its roots—make it subject to infestation, gaseous injury, or a rude cut that never heals? What is the point of its evolution into death? When can we say that evolution has begun? I cannot mean to say that I can see its dying any more than I can see its death. So I must deny that I can actually see its life, or, let me be grand as well as outrageous, and say that I can know very little about the intricate relations of its being. We find analogy at this point debilitating.

We find conceptualization onerous. Someone will argue, as folk have for centuries, that language gives us body, and that the more complex the language the more complex the body. Now, here we sit, trying to give depth and shape to death, to make it a concept that displays its complexity. But we are trapped by our inability to give substance to individuality and the complexity that individuality requires. We almost, in order to be able to say anything about the dimensions we claim to have uncovered when we speak of death, have to return to a logical operation. Intuition tells us to scurry from such an operation, without giving in to a debilitating and unrewarding form of mysticism. We have drawn close to what might be an insoluble problem.

We know we cannot submit this interrogation of death's dimensions to a logical operation; yet we know that we have an obligation to substantiate a phenomenon that can only be approached concretely, but one that resists the boundaries we presume to know. How can we frame the dilemma? We know what we sense, and yet we do not sense what we know. Or, we sense what we know, but do not know what we sense. We cannot settle the question by turning it into a problem in epistemology, or set the question aside by making it an ontological notion that requires neither solution nor comment.

I see now, too, how far we have come from an appeal to language. Irony of ironies, the familiar tolling starts. I catch myself before I go cascading into contradiction. Death's context is not in language. This investigation proceeds because we want to determine just where that context lies. We must say it again, and say it more simply: we intend, we can only intend, to establish death's domain and, in doing so, come upon an understanding of newly constructed relationships.

As we go, it might seem that this pilgrim revels in divestiture. Earlier on, it appeared that terms would proliferate beyond accountability or even utility. Now, it appears that this text suffers from the threat of being thoroughly without linguistic resources, deboned of any epistemological structure. Is that a necessary, or salutary, consequence of this type of inquiry? We ask ourselves whether it is necessary or desirable to be so definitionally astringent, placing our closure at the beginning of the beginning. But how is it possible to follow every line of inquiry suggested by a resident body that has never been fully apprehended or comprehensively questioned? We proceed, and confront, and negotiate with impossibilities.

Have we reached absurdity? Can the pilgrim really mean to suggest that death is an impossibility, or at best a negotiation that the mind, or the spirit, or something unperceived or misconceived, undertakes?

I perhaps have spent too much time around Peter Galison's books and essays, and have been too much influenced by his way with domain analysis, and I mean to say here, his idea of the inevitable, necessary, creative and salutary negotiation involved when practitioners in separate domains cross the borders. But why shouldn't we see negotiation as a functional impulse (I almost said, variable) in, or within, two domains that we usually and inexplicably keep separate? Passing, I notice that

I have said, happily, negotiation within the domains. I have to address that with-inness at some point, but must hold it apart from a primary discussion—that of the negotiation we can specify between life and death.

We approach an uninstructive point here when we speak of life and death. The words, if not the events, are too often conjoined. We seem to rest content with our unimpeachable observation that one mode of existence ceases when the other begins. We feel wise because we do not go beyond observing their propulsive conjunction, and we feel courageous for having faced up to them as they are, or, I should say, as we think they are. We do not, understandably, want to create problems by asking what would seem absurd questions, bringing into play notions not normally associated with either mode and certainly not normally associated with the two modes in conjunction. We want simplicity. A body, a being, is alive, or it is dead. An entity is living or it's dying. The deep ones among us will insist that we are all, and always, dying from the moment of our birth. We must acknowledge the justice in such an assertion, while at the same time insisting that the assertion does not carry us very far. Speaking in the voices of the deep ones, we can say that, yes, life implies movement within, the constant negotiation of growth and decay. But here we are trying to go beyond a primary observation, a first understanding, and we need to subject our clear and simple ideas to further inquiry.

What can we possibly mean by negotiation with regard to life and death? What could each offer to the other?

We might begin by saying that life could offer death a future. Would I have been more exact if I had said the possibility of a future? Wouldn't that be another begging of the question, pretending that death could be held off and established only as a possibility? You might insist that the real question-begging lies not in asserting the possibility of death but in ignoring the inevitability of death. We *must* have the recognition that we, all phenomena, die. That has to define the existence we here bring into question. But no, our approach suggests that life remains the primary possibility, and we can conceive of an absence that need not submit itself to our inquiry. Put simply, it is possible not to have come into existence. In such a case, there would be nothing to have a future; it would be absurd to speak of the culmination of a process that has no beginning; it would be absurd to speak of the potential of a form that by definition cannot be specified.

We feel that we have walked too far into abstraction. We seem to have walked away from singularity, from individuality, from the specific and proper case. Even if we shy from arguing universals, we must acknowledge that all we know (some would say, all that we can know) depends upon the individual and very specific case. We do not have to do a mathematical calculation, starting at one, to determine that we are surrounded by life. Life confronts us in its actuality, not in its possibility. If we think of the possibility of nonbeing, we have already entered upon a consideration of death. We cannot transform dead bodies into nonbeing nor think of nonbeing as the beginning of a process that leads to death. We cannot say with any assurance how we do proceed from the recognition of a living body to the recognition that some boundary between being and nonbeing has been overcome. That failure forces us to approach the notion of possibility with more trepidation, and makes us reexamine the idea of a future.

We have involved ourselves in a tangle of motives. We keep skirting the problem of time; we have no logical demonstration of time's efficacy in solving any of the problems that we can now associate with possibility or the future. We should be

uneasy in speaking of *the future*. We might say that we have in-
troduced an insoluble complication by speaking of the multidi-
mensionality of life and death. To be scrupulous, to bring this
definable tense, the future, into our purview, we ought to allow
the multidimensionality of the future, meaning that we cannot
speak of the future but of futures. Nothing says that doing that
will tell us anything of any use about the relationship of an in-
dividual life to its own individual death. I want to say that we
assume that individuals have individual and differing futures,
and I want to complicate that assumption by asserting that each
individual proceeds through several and variable futures. Now,
if we ask, can life offer death a future, we find ourselves con-
founded by a simplicity that cannot be realized.

Where is the flaw? Can it be in treating life as an attribute
of individuals or, in error, turning individuals into an attribute
of life? We proceed by an unpremeditated return, and yet we
cannot speak of first principles; we cannot erase these difficul-
ties by definition. Has our move to clear this domain faltered
on the idea of negotiation? We keep turning around an implica-
tion of relation, as concept and as active force between life and
death.

Donald Davidson, in a paper treating the irreducibility of
the concept of the self, admits that, in order to talk about this
problem, he has to address it indirectly. That pretty much is
where I find myself with respect to the relation that compels
my attention. We cannot find a direct line to the reality of such
a relation. We recognize a need to take some things for granted,
to accept some clearly defined notions as established, such as
the one we have just introduced, reality. A skeptical bone tells
us not to do that; analytical pride forces us to want an unim-
peachable rigor. We want the words we use to be free of suspi-
cion. But here we ask, who would, who has, cast suspicion on

notions that allow us to go forward, that sanction our investigation and help us to broaden the sphere, not only of our investigation but our experience? However we handle the question of irreducibility, we remain uneasy with the idea of proceeding obliquely toward even a tentative resolution of our problem.

You will say that we have got ourselves in a fix. We move forward with life's generosity; we suggest an exchange. We appear to have tried death's passivity, or to put it another way, to have attributed a passivity to death because life, in the instance we have just proposed, confers a future upon death. Color us not cantankerous when we suggest that we can begin from the other end and consider that death offers a future to life.

Looking at things this way controls our notion of time, and again we seem unprepared to address time's place in the relationship we have proposed. We want, in effect, to run away from the future, or to put it under erasure while addressing the perhaps insoluble relation of life and death. Surely, negotiation offers us a wide range of event, transactions between parties concerned to inhabit (we might say, share) the same ground. We have to take into account that negotiation also involves exclusion, a thinning that almost belies the apparent enhancement each party realizes. We meet with the idea that a negotiator in the process of negotiation is inevitably transformed, we might even say transfigured and risk the theological implication involved in doing so.

You will have noticed that we have slipped negotiation's reality past the gate of reality in itself. We played tricky with the future, but we insist upon continuing with the multifaceted process of negotiation. Why? It gives us a chance to talk about fertile notions, such as divestment and transformation, exclusion, inclusion, resistance and acceptance.

In the process of considering divestment, we can play stupid if we want, take the easy road. Imagine what seems a transparent conclusion that a person who dies has been divested of life, dispossessed of certain attributes we have to pretend to understand, that is, we think we have an understanding of what constitutes life. We must leave aside, for the moment, the complicated problem of a singular expression for life. We agree that every living entity will bundle its attributes toward that goal, that unique expression we can call life. In a sense, we divest life of those unmarked attributes that might define life. We might almost be said to be thinking negatively, constructing a nonexistent realm that makes the forms of our attention upon life possible. We create a strange situation—divestment has become a requirement, a logic, of possibility (and perhaps we could take this notion to its extreme limits and say, the probability of life). We almost stumble into an absurdity: dispossession of nonexistent attributes secures the possession of qualities that determine life. Our argument strives here to avoid coming to terms, again, at this point, with the idea that various forms of life might (we almost said, must) display differing attributes that make it possible, in each individual case, to declare that we have a life before us. This would complicate our consideration of dispossession. Put simply, all life, and I phrase it in this way to insist upon a necessary generality, might play among various formal attributes and varying forms of divestment. We might think of ourselves as playing among the probabilities of a life in possession of its proper attributes and the contending probabilities of that life being stripped of those attributes. We realize that we talk as though we would want to say divestment means taking any, in the sense of loss. Suppose, though, that we mean divestment as a freeing impulse, a liberating enhancement of existence, turning a body toward its entanglement with death? This brings us to the paradox of welcoming the return of that bundle, that nonexistent realm we had thought to discard.

We thought divestment, and thought we could proceed by addressing a transparent conclusion, but find ourselves tempted, if not foolishly encouraged, to pursue notions that seem even more absurd than the ones we have proposed. I might have taken advantage of a move that allows me to pursue such absurdity, exchanging the terms divestment and dispossession, as though one were the translation of the other, as, in fact, we seem to understand. I have to focus upon dispossession as the operative term because that allows me to count upon the implication of possession. I need such linguistic trickery to address another fertile notion suggested by an act of dispossession; that notion is transformation.

Can we say that we can ever dispossess a body of an attribute by transforming that attribute, translating it into an altogether different entity? One might say that transformation has a value, while dispossession seems a thoroughly negative enterprise, and that such a translation would be senseless and useless. We think of transformation's positive value because we always think of transformation as a fully achieved act, a definitive move from one state to another, a substitution of one state for another where nothing remains of the prior state whose attributes can have no effect upon the new and realized state. But are we justified in thinking this way? Is there no residue of the prior state, something that not only determines the quality but that enhances our perception of and our abilities to use the current state? By asking these questions, we seem to be recalling that notion of entanglement we have noted.

What in the world can it mean to speak of death as a state we can use? We stopped along this way to address divestment, got ourselves thoroughly entangled in trying to account for

transformation, and have begun to treat the terms of our nego-
tiation, or should I say, the terms of a negotiation we want ap-
parently to find between life and death, as transparent, to such
an extent that we have spoken of the quality of a state, states, we
remain unable to define. We have compounded this confusion
by speaking of enhancement of properties that we take to be
involved in an irresolvable relation, and have arrived at the im-
possible notion of being able to use death.

There is, though, good reason to proceed along this path.
We have tried to establish divestment as a liberating enhance-
ment of existence. We have insisted upon divestment's, or dis-
possession's, involvement with transformation, that is, transfor-
mation as a defining act that remains fluid. I insist that we can
think of these two processes as qualities that allow us access to
the deep, authentic qualities of life and death. We can speak of
using death, as we can of using life, in the sense that they com-
pel investigation into being itself. Use, by this measure, has been
given exploratory value, and has thrown us into the danger of a
wakefulness we might have refused.

One might ask, could we use something other than death?
or life?—abstractions too impossible to contain. There could
perhaps be other fundamental negotiations we could establish
and explore. We could, and probably would, have far more suc-
cess in displaying our ingenuity, but ingenuity is not the point;
consciousness is, and remains so. So we speak to death, and
negotiate its complex relationship to life to uncover another
relationship that on its own might not reveal itself. You say re-
lationship. You say consciousness. Where is the paradigm? To
what does consciousness respond? And isn't this unremitting
attention to that other negotiation simply a blind and blinding
mistake? These questions make me acknowledge a momentary
pause, and call attention to a perhaps debilitating blindness. My

consciousness might not, in this instance, respond to my blindness, or engage me in some paradigmatic ingenuity. One does not go tweaking death's nature and form to contain it. There is no paradigm to establish by searching death or its companionship with life, or by searching the elaborate and free-flowing body called consciousness. Pursuing death, you will embrace it. Coming into life's domain you will play with a body that runs away from you. I could distress you by asserting that consciousness might recoil from your touch. And yet we must be faithful to these dangers. Faithful to the vibrancy in the exclusion I have proposed.

We move from one outrageous proposal to another. We come to dispossession's rough edge, transformation's knotty interior. We try to keep our eye on that multifaceted process, called negotiation, but find ourselves called away from that meditation to attend to another engagement. If dispossession is indeed a form of freedom, we ought to be intoxicated with a concomitant freedom. I feel queasy about calling into being an attribute that seems trivial, meek, mocking. What makes me scramble after the idea of exclusion as a mark of such freedom I have proposed? Why not walk by the idea that to dispossess someone or something means to exclude some aspect of that particular being? Isn't it possible to approach, to see, this dispossessed being in what would appear a pristine state, that is, without even the intuition that some property has been set aside?

We can get silly about this. Let us say that we have a death before us. We recognize a dispossession. Some voice will raise itself against my attributing the idea of freedom to death, as I will have done by seeing death as dispossession. Someone will argue that it makes no sense to talk of a necessary exclusion when we have no evidence of a necessary existence of any property we might pretend to analyze. No one feels the need to argue that it is inane to talk of the loss of a property that was never there. Thorough subtlety can charm us. Disingenuous subtlety can lead us astray. I must hear the clamor inevitably arising around the notion of that entanglement which makes exclusion a notable force, an instance, some might argue, of that disingenuous subtlety. Nevertheless, I insist that exclusion constitutes a part of that necessary freedom we encounter in dispossession. I will argue that we must understand exclusion as a process in which we are involved systematically in thinking about death (to restrict ourselves here to thinking about death). I mean to say here, too, that writing "systematically" should call our attention to our thinking as thinking of a system, meaning that these elements we are now proposing—such as dispossession, transformation, exclusion, inclusion—are components of a complex process whether we notice or understand this complex in its transparent or hidden forms (and I must speak of forms).

There, I have edged further into my argument for entanglement. Intuition tells us, and my proceeding through this questioning of the complex relationship, life and death, asks us to think in the plural. I would be unboundedly outrageous, and say that we can take what I have said about exclusion as an example of this systematic involvement. The body, let's say, does not want to take on more attributes than it can use, and a living body, in the process of that negotiation we are trying to define, remains attuned to an ungraspable element, and the element under scrutiny here, exclusion, will affirm its weight by its absence.

We seem caught in a contradiction. Can absent, or nonexistent, entities display weight? Can they have any effect upon a process that is, by its nature, observable, measurable? We circle these questions, and perhaps circle and evade the task of defining what might ultimately be singularly simple. We ask ourselves whether we should pursue a composition or a decomposition.

Can I really be asking you to make a choice of procedure? Could I leave things like that, and pretend to advance a rigorous methodology, getting the terms straight, making necessary distinctions, preening ourselves upon having found the A and B of a logical argument? But would it make any sense to choose between addressing life, or death, as a composition, or addressing life, or death, as a decomposition? We think we could talk succinctly about life, if we only spoke of its composition, thereby giving it empirical definition. We could, on the other hand, speak of its decomposition, a gradual disintegration, an erosion of powers. I enter upon a dangerous area, and declare that this is not the choice I ask you to make. I mean to encourage us to accept a different cut, one having to do with exclusion. We work hard here to avoid a simple equation: cut equals exclusion. We move imaginatively to bring the idea of exclusion along a different path that leads us to see how it makes sense to think of being cut into life or, what I won't argue at the moment, being cut into death. I will insist upon our being given the opportunity to realize a possibility that did not exist prior to our consciousness of it, that indefinable moment when you awaken to that set of circumstances that tells you you are alive, or dead. I understand that you might feel that here I am being impossibly refined, buffing a trivial notion into significance.

But I cannot let the notion of choosing to be aware of a particular form of existence go unexamined. It might help to think of my version of the cut not as a cutting away but as a shaping, a way of giving form. We need only think of what we take to be a similar process in art. We have heard often enough, when someone speaks of an artist's accomplishment, she knows what to leave out. So we have exclusion, but we need to remember that we think the thing in hand has been shaped by choice. Can we cross this border, perhaps too easily, and imagine that life in itself admits of what I will call first-order choosing, and mean by that that a consciousness admits—should I say, permits?—an awareness of a possible existence, shaped by what its form seems to exclude? Outrage enough? I will go further, and claim that what we can here understand through these propositions about life holds if we treat death.

We have given exclusion such a prominent place in our discussion that to speak now of inclusion might strike us as absurd. Need we fuss with the attributes of inclusion in order to fix our concepts of life and death? We pretend we have satisfied one set of claims by a persuasion to accept the realized claims of a set of circumstances we seem to have made the first term in a binary opposition. We might think exclusion as opposed to inclusion, the body present as opposed to the body absent. But our argument works to try to establish that we cannot use such a binary opposition and cannot see the body present and the body absent as anything if not entangled.

We keep skipping around certain notions, such as detachment, which the idea of exclusion and of inclusion brings to mind, and place. A body, living or dead, must have a place, some point upon which it rests, or from which it moves. But there we have the difficulty of thinking of place as a point or a set of points, and we ease further into difficulty by thinking that a body can be detached from its place. Before we pursue detachment, we face another question we probably would like to avoid. Should we think of a body in its place as a body resting in singular space? Or can we think of a body as inhabiting a many-valued space? And I might even suggest that we have been busy keeping bodies in motion, tying them to the activities that surround and sustain them. That is a long-winded way of saying that an individual body needs the relation of other existent bodies—to be perhaps too plain about it, a body needs, for example, the resistance of air, the resistance of its own internal processes to the constitutive processes that lie outside the body. So all is movement; all is a process of a body detaching itself from place in order to inhabit the potential world of place or, to take this notion to its limits, to define and to redefine the inhabitable potential of place and, in doing so, to make of its internal processes a manifold construction, a constitution, of place.

We seem always to be effecting a return to some point we have left. At this point, you might be struck by what I will call a hidden variable. Our argument examines a form of existence, that is to say, it seeks an understanding of constitutive processes that speak to us of life and death. Where does the variable lie? What is hidden? If we reflect for a moment, we sense a presence we appear to have obscured—an audience.

What do we gain by introducing such an absurd complement to this discussion at this point? We think we have established the body present and, by implication, the body absent. We insist upon a certain cut into significance with regard to those bodies. We can even entertain the idea of place and its attendant property, detachment. We need not now pursue the plausibility of exclusion, inclusion, resistance and acceptance as engagements with form. Still, something itches. We could be naïve and ask, where do the questions go? Who is concerned with this puzzle we have summoned? Some misunderstanding, perhaps of intent, provokes us to say that the body present cannot be its own audience. That thought strikes us as error. The conscious body must indeed be its own audience. You contend that that might be true, if we mean Sarah or Saul, or the fawn that is just now crossing the lawn, or the hummingbird at the butterfly bush. We must attribute a form of consciousness to all entities capable of movement. We pull rapidly away from an investigation of will, from any idea of a self-directed impulse that would lead us to make that oak we dispatched a reasoning ens and, god forbid, our equal. The question of audience becomes too tricky. It leads away from the many forms of existence we have struggled to establish. But there remains a virtue in thinking of audience as an entity's focused and singular attention to its presence and to its inevitable movement toward its death.

What are we proposing? that it takes an audience to confirm the body present and the body absent? that the constitutive potential of place only matters when there is a refutation, some force or being that can, in principle, deny these bodies' existence? We seem to suggest that a body's ability to deny its own existence is the mark of its existence. How far will that take us? Far enough to be brought face to face with the idea: so with life, so with death. If you can conceive of your nonexistence, can you not conceive of denying your own death? I want to phrase this in its most outrageous fashion: can't you conceive that death does not exist? What happens to our entanglement?

What we are asking is that death come into existence, submit itself to examination. Death might accommodate us, but, in doing so, it has to violate its individuality, for it can only enter into our examination as part of the configuration we have tried to establish. Why now ask it to stand apart so that we can search it for hidden attributes? We come to a point where we meet ourselves turning the corner of existence to find that we have encountered a fundamental problem—to account for the existence and inevitability of death. We cannot pretend that we can simply walk by this problem, take death for granted, treat it as though it were the only form of existence that fits on the other side of that form we call life. If we proceed in this way, we are, in effect, playing in and with that logic we thought we had abandoned. Yet we find that we are forced to look for a third, perhaps indefinable form of existence that would have some effect upon the forms we have proposed.

Should we now give up and give in to an unexamined notion? Life seems no more than possible. We might even go further, and speak of life as a matter of probability, almost effacing ourselves in the unbridgeable world of probability. Someone sits, as I do now, and fiddles with a recalcitrant pen, distressed by the rough passage of thought to hand with the pen, annoyed with the ink that doesn't flow. What form of existence controls this negotiation? We must despair of ever untangling the phenomena that make such a simple act such a complex frustration, an unspecifiable bundle of cellular possibilities (say not, probabilities), which cannot be encompassed in a singular notion of existence we can only call life. A moment ago, we were proposing resistance as a criterion for life. But that was a concern of bodies, of the familiar bodies capable of conception, growth and decay. It would be absurd to say the pen falls into this category. Recall, though, that earlier we wanted to think differently about domain and how a body's extended domain helped to shape a form of existence. If, now, we turn back to death's individuality, we feel shamed by our inability to compose that face, undone by our failure to identify the manifold relationships of the many forms of existence. We have counted upon life's generosity, but we seem not to have been instructed in its cautions. This circumstance makes us return to entanglement. We do so because addressing entanglement seems the only way to say anything of any consequence about death.

Why should this be so? Why can't we subscribe to a third form of existence that would have nothing to do with death but

that would enter upon the same form of entanglement with life
that we have given to life and death? Why should we not see a
universe of entangled forms? That would, we think, do away
with death's individuality. But there you catch us; you claim,
correctly, that though we have been busy chasing death's indi-
viduality, we have not by any means established it. That failure
calls up a more expensive one—the failure to establish life's
individuality, meaning the failure to establish that only an indi-
vidual life can lead to the kind of entanglement (if we can so
phrase it) that makes sense of the complex negotiation we have
under scrutiny.

In effect, we have buried death's individuality by calling
up an entanglement of all phenomena. You will argue that we
have become too clever by half, escaping a necessary evalua-
tion of existence by simply observing a world, a universe, of
phenomena, and accepting its presence as evidence enough of
its existence. Inscribing that sentence required another look.
I realized that the universe could not be the subject of our
inquiry. We must be concerned with the phenomena that we
believe compose that universe, and, if we count ourselves
scrupulous, we would have to count upon and record the in-
dividual attributes of each one of those phenomena. You
claim, as you might, that this is disingenuous, a further eva-
sion. Here we are, trying to say something complete about
death as a phenomenon that orders a form of existence, and
arguing that we can find a disencumbrance that would justify
such a generality, yet find ourselves brought up short because
we cannot definitively assert the necessary being and particu-
larity of the two phenomena we have chosen to explore in their
relational existence. Have we come this far only to end accepting
the relational value of everything? What do we need? A version
of a theory of light? Something we could use to measure all

event, every collision, within that complex relationship we isolate for investigation?

We have run into a wall. We chase a formal construction that seems to tell us nothing about an actual construction, meaning that we cannot be sure that we are dealing with an actually existing phenomenon and have not allowed our imagination to create a set of possible events that we can set spinning in the universe simply by giving those events names. We track gently around the entanglement we have defined for these particular events, and hope that no undefined, or ill-defined, set of events appears to confound this particular entanglement. Here is the knot: we have conceived a misconception by admitting that we have not uncovered necessity.

Certainly, it sounds silly to say the man does not know if he is alive or dead. I argue that that is not the ultimate absurdity or the one that confronts us now. We might ask, does the man know that he is something other than alive or dead? Can we frame another form of existence? Can we begin the ordering of a lexicon in which we find a meaning for the phrase, "otherwise than being"? Mucking about in that lexicon might make it seem that we are arguing with a transcendental ontology or a Levinasian argument with essence. But I want to encourage a ruthlessness that goes beyond seeing ourselves as the point of existence and as the only negotiators, or should I say, the only subjects capable of a negotiation, or, going further, the only capable subjects of a negotiation we have defined. You will tread upon such ill-bred refinement. You will suggest that I cannot even conceive what would bring about the negotiation, the formulative events, that involve the growth and emptying of that oak we might soon dispatch. Our relationship to the oak is not here at play. We will get nowhere with analogy. We seek an understanding of an ontological form that might not have surfaced. Being unacquainted, or at least ill-at-ease with the form, we cannot ascertain its applicability, or its place, in a universe of forms. We continue to go from outrage to outrage. If you follow me along this path, you will see that I have involved us in a universe of potential and perhaps indefinable forms.

This is a hell of a way to proceed. We start trying to understand death and existence; we break off to ask about other forms of existence; and end by asking if existence can be called by another name, by other names. The term, *existence*, seems to travel on common sense. We say, I exist, you exist, Buenos Aires exists, the Sonora Desert exists, the peacock exists. We find it easy to extend the range of existence. Our imagination might insist that angels exist, or God exists, or that there is an existent spirit, growing out of the emptiness within us. We never pause to examine these declarations; we would be embarrassed by the evidence before us. I am not opening that box of tattered arguments for the appearance and substance of phenomena. We will not, at this point, set off to prove God's existence, or work energetically to establish our own. Someone might contend that we have bound ourselves irrevocably by proposing a fundamental act that we have called negotiation long before we had unequivocally established the properties we would accept as evidence of life's or death's existence. We ran with an ordinary acceptance of such properties. We let ourselves be carried away by a fundamental need to have a subject and a desire to account for a complexity of motives guided by what we thought unimpeachable perceptions.

Our investigation wants to retreat. We keep winding ourselves into difficulties because we cannot accept any complex of attributes that would tell us that we had exhaustively defined our subjects. Perhaps our greatest difficulty might reside in our inability to insist upon the truth of our perceptions. I hear your laughter. Would we have these difficulties if we hadn't proposed death as our most capable cohort? Or if we had not declared our intention to examine death as though it were as complex as what we understand as life? We need not speak of mystery. But uncovering a disequilibrium in our perception of death we have uncovered a disequilibrium in our perception of life, and have made that particular entanglement worthy of our regard because it leads away from itself, not by analogy but by methodological implication to domains that lie apart from that entanglement.

What have we done to ourselves? Were we, in fact, after an assured explication of those discernible events, life and death? We certainly do not have that. We seem only to have occasioned a proliferation of questions about the relations of any and all events, to bring into question the notion of an intrinsic conscious life. We struggle with the proper way to state this proposition because we have had to refer not only to consciousness but to life, the very point under scrutiny—that is to say, we treat the subjectivity we claimed as a fundamental need. Oh, you caught me. Shouldn't we, in order to be scrupulous, speak of an intrinsic conscious death? Don't accuse me of playing games in opposition to a voice that has only briefly appeared here. I work hard to keep these pages free of an exegesis, or a questioning, of the specific subjective consciousness we find in Levinas. I want to go beyond the notion that an unperceived material thing can only be its capability of being perceived.

I want to enter that universe of potential and perhaps indefinable forms to ask whether the material existence of such forms is not an inherent attribute that remains impervious of our perception. Perhaps we ride toward disaster. But let us suppose the existence of forms that do not rely upon any definition of existence we have so far proposed; in other words, we might suppose that they respond to (or, if you want, we might grasp them by) other names—other names that mirror our understanding of existence but are not our understanding of existence, but terms (if we must have terms) that speak of the process of growth and decay, transformative possibility, we have given to the term, *existence*. That complication takes us far beyond any need to argue for the appearance and substance of phenomena.

Surely, you exclaim, this cannot be what you mean by *acceptance*, a term you left in abeyance while exploring dispossession? How then can these indefinable forms find or participate in the creative possibilities you discern in dispossession? How can they display this dispossession, or be said to have anything of which to be dispossessed? We all seem complicit in denying these other forms (and we feel compelled to harbor this terminological awkwardness) any consciousness. We must have accepted that consciousness means being continually present to oneself. Tell me about the proliferation of difficulties. Would it ever be possible to speak of "oneself" with regard to these forms? Our ideas of individuality, of oneself, rely upon our conception of subjectivity, and subjectivity remains an attribute we reserve for beings who display our form of existence. You will notice the hesitation here. I am reluctant to argue for an expansive range of subjectivity; to say this perhaps too bluntly, I waffle in trying to specify subjectivity. Why do I walk around this problem? Why can't I say that we have no way of addressing the subjectivity of a hummingbird, or a fisher cat, even if we think that the bird, or the cat, is capable of consciousness as we pretend to understand it? As I say this, I draw us closer to the rougher point I set out to make. We do not have, and probably cannot have, entry into the consciousness of the indefinable forms I have introduced as a challenge; indeed, we can have very little conception (I almost said, cannot have any idea) of whether these forms need the operation of consciousness.

Why make such a fuss over these points? Why barrel about these gardens in search of distinctive definitions? What is the hidden argument? Are we trying to tie these forms of existence to our own forms of existence, bring them into the domain where what we determine about life and death and that peculiar entanglement will speak clearly, be determinative, of all forms of existence, even if we have to confront an inscrutable form or an absence? You might say that we work much too hard to declare our ignorance. We seem at work upon an emptying of concepts, a creative and innovative stripping of the consciousness that would make the body present and the body absent possible. We might discover that, at bottom, what we are arguing with is our conception of the transformative possibilities of forms of existence, calling into question that congenial negotiation we felt obtained between life and death. Earlier, we spoke only of finding a third form. We did not feel the need to insist upon a proliferation of forms. Now, we seem to need a proliferation of forms to display the complexity of our primary entanglement, and to demonstrate that nothing in our experience of that entanglement suggests that we can ever have anything other than an intuitive and incomplete understanding of life's, and thereby death's, dimensions.

All of this canter through the fields of other forms intends only to make us uneasy, unsure of the value of dimension. What disastrous arrogance. We seem to have given up on our abilities to measure death's dimensions. Measuring those would, we thought, certainly give us access to those hidden dimensions in that other domain. Now, we seem to declare that death can have no dominion, and no dimension. Why have we turned against our own intuition? Shall we call this turning a failure? Can we even begin to explain such a failure? Perhaps. Intuition, insight, takes courage. Suppose we bind our courage to the sticking place, and pursue death into its many dimensions. We should pause to say that, before we have set out upon that task, we have already made one courageous determination. We have taken life's multidimensionality as given, and we had to do this because we needed a system of dimensionality by which to measure any other, even if we overlook any disjunction or incongruity in treating differing entities within the same sphere. An uneasiness might soon surface. Turning against our intuition is one failure, but turning dimension into a necessity might represent a greater failure. Suppose, for a moment, that death resists taking on the dimensions we have ascribed to it and remains a singularly simple phenomenon. You will have noticed that we cannot prescribe the form of resistance we might handily acknowledge. You may fairly accuse me of having circumscribed death's field of action in order to speak of resistance, and you might have seen that resistance implies the existence of dimensions that go beyond any surface dimension. We cannot find the simplicity that would obviate consideration of complexity. We seem urged toward a larger vision, and within that vision we find that we need to follow the unfolding of a process—that is to say, necessity resides in that unfolding; we insist that the unfolding comprises the necessity we require.

We burrow deeper into our difficulties. We turn on ourselves. We cast aside perfectly plausible conclusions to scout the other side of an argument we thought we had overcome. Page after page, we have traversed a labyrinth of motives, focused upon a singular goal, freedom, as it expresses itself in the process and quality of two fundamental forms of existence. How can we possibly find freedom in the form of necessity we have defined? Or maybe that is not the way to frame the question. Perhaps it should be, how have we arrived at a point where we equate freedom and necessity, see them as complementary processes? Someone will have seen through the primary maneuver, that moment when we linked life and death as complementary guardians of the ground of being. Even one so alert will not confuse this hunting of the ground of being with those notions of that ground that we associate with Tillich, or any other form that grows from a theological impulse. The critic might absolve us of a theological impulse and make no fuss over the skirting of authority, that is, the impulse to acknowledge authority, even as its grounds for being slip disturbingly out of sight.

Again, we come upon a moment of apparent rest that should disturb. What have we done? We have given death an authority as creative, as determinative, as capable of transformative power, as life. We notice how meager our regard of life's attributes appears. Have we taken too much for granted? How can we keep insisting on entanglement, when one form of that linkage seems the definitive authority within that linkage? Long ago, we did away with hierarchy in our inquiry and, by that act, ought to have done away with authority. Say that we do not know how to order our inquiry because we have found no way to follow the process we claim to have under investigation. We do not know where we enter upon this inquiry; we do not even know where we begin as existent bodies. Can I say that last with even more astringency: we know nothing consequential about the birth of our being. Rephrase it for emphasis: each of us knows nothing consequential about the birth of being, as process or accomplished act. You cry that the pilgrim seems set on not understanding being as an attribute of a universe that existed as a presence before it realized its significance, if that realization is even possible. We find ourselves being drawn further into an acknowledgment of those indefinable forms that would complete our universe of being.

I refuse, riding my uneasiness, to elevate being into Being. You might sense a retreat from, some would call it a confusion over, the term Being's, extensive domain. We cannot talk of beyond Being, if we cannot come to terms with Being. But what is gained by the lowercase presentation of being? Have we done away with the problems arising from material existence? Have we even discovered a way to propose material existence? And, going further, can we offer anything regarding that supposedly indefinable realm we will call beyond being? We argue with ourselves, feeling the need to complete our universe of existent beings even though we remain blind to innumerable constitutive elements that lie out of reach. Think of these constitutive elements as dark matter. We shy from asserting that what the physicist understands as a primary constituent of the universe is the same element helping us to define the being we search. The physicist's dark matter is potentially measurable; intuition tells us that those constitutive elements we would stand beside our fundamental entanglement cannot be so easily measured. We have to insist upon such a distinction because we need distinction, some perspective from which to view the thoroughgoing processes involved in life and death, and in their entanglement. If we were to submit those indefinable existent forms to the same formal analysis that we undertake, have undertaken, with life and death, we will have accomplished a formal maneuver but will have allowed a real presence, unmanageable by such an analysis, to escape.

A question returns. What makes us so sure that these "dark matter" forms exist? Why do we hold so fast to the idea that it is possible to use the idea of these forms in a way that illuminates our entanglement without those forms being contaminated by that entanglement? Earlier on, we edged toward suggesting death's primary authority. Now, we seem to edge toward asserting the primary and overriding authority of those indefinable forms of existence. You could call me to account, play Humean, and ask me to justify the real presence of an ens, a complex of entities (one struggles to find a useful term) that will not even register a wobble upon its revolution through our universe of real presences that life and death can display. Ah, you sigh, it's that old mystery that encompasses our being and act, and compels us to acknowledge the gaps not only in our knowledge but in our existence. Perhaps this is why our investigation has been oriented more toward an understanding of death, its processes and attributes, than toward life's processes and attributes, given the entanglement we have proposed. We say without saying that what we cannot orient defines us as much as, or more than, what we can.

But, then, have we been trying to make it possible to define a form of existence, or trying to make it possible to step outside existence, to negate the several forms of existence without undoing the idea of existence? Others would now speak of consciousness, and offer that as a resolution to the problem that has surfaced.

Is this a job that consciousness can do? Someone will want to push another question. Can we find that consciousness? I once in another context reduced consciousness to the patches and tubes of a material body, which is no more than to say that I thought consciousness inconceivable without some form of material existence. If we follow that line, we have to give up the idea of stepping outside existence because, without the body that occupies a conceivable space, an ens (and here I have to stay with this ugly construction to keep the idea of the other than human present) can have nothing from which to step away. As they might say in the local pub, that plays hell with our notion of indefinable forms. We cannot see the nothing we have given them for their domain, and cannot speculate upon the particular mobility that brings these forms into being. We find ourselves whirling through a labyrinth of questions that cannot be expressed as a labyrinth of possibilities. To a particular form of nothingness we struggle to attribute a necessary reality. But we intuit that we have not necessarily advanced into reality, and we feel almost undone because we sense that we might be falling into an apparent domain that was explored, mapped and abandoned. We fight vivaciously to keep from a repetitive investigation of reality; we fight to resist the idea that reality is the question. We almost seem set upon denying that reality and consciousness have anything to do with formal existence. There again we run aground. Is it that we can only accept formal existence, that is, accept form as the only mode of existence? What could we mean if we said indefinable existent, with no intimation of form? How could we divest ourselves of the idea of form and remain conversant with the idea of existence? Here we go again, entering the labyrinth that goes nowhere near death's domain. Have we subtly made death an indefinable existent, and then compounded a problem by adhering to the entanglement we have defined, making, in effect, life an indefinable existent?

Let's talk about contamination. These little observables, life and death, show themselves by their activity (I almost want to speak the way Feynman spoke about the birds; it doesn't matter what we call them, what matters is that we understand what they do), and they might give evidence of their existence by their very obscurity and their abilities to provoke the activity of other entities. We argue that neither can remain pure; they become contaminated by their activity and by, we say, their entanglement. This argument now goes further by insisting that contamination in this regard is not only provocative but creative. You will notice that we have reasoned from an alien process—that small contamination of matter the physicists discern in the early universe. You might sense a larger problem, a larger necessary development—we might have to find the early universe of life and death. We know that would be an intellectual accomplishment. But what assurances could we draw from that achievement with respect to the contemporary existence of life and death?

This search for evidence for the early universe of life and death involves us in something approaching treachery to our investigation. We feel that we have labored through these pages, seeking a security that we could only get by treating the complex, life, in a manner that implicitly acknowledges its priority of being in the special relationship we are pursuing, or have pursued. Shall we be outrageous again? We have taken life as our guide, that is, we have adopted that complex, life, as the inadvertent standard for the other complex, death, that concerns us here. We always begin with life and insist, by doing so, that every other process submits to its command. But what if we were to begin with death? Could we, or should we, direct our attention to a different set of markers, and examine death as though it grew from an early universe that did not depend upon the complex we have always taken for a standard? Doing so asks us to understand that death might be playing by rules we have never understood because our existential vocabulary has always been inadequate, unable to define the processes that make death what it is. How easy is it to start again, searching a sphere that, just as the physicist's universe, is still in process? Our cosmologists have determined, by measuring the activity of this particular universe, that the universe continues to expand. We think that we have found an exemplum. We speak of death's universe. So we are encouraged to speak of death's infinite expansion. How can such knowledge enlighten us? The question does not seem to be, how does death expand, or transform itself? We need first to know, one might argue, how such a universe could have arisen without elemental connections and activities of prior existent forms. Or, we have to accept that death is sui generis and cannot be explained, or forthrightly understood. We have to understand it, in that case, as something that acts upon the other beings in a universe that can only be seen as a parallel universe. That means that these beings can have no effect, no influence, upon a process whose effects are everywhere evident in what we are calling the parallel universe. We cannot have such a notion. We want to draw, we need to draw, these complexes into the same domain because we cannot conceive of any universe devoid of negotiation.

So what have we determined, that exchange is the only value of our entanglement? Ought we be bold enough to insist that exchange is the only value of existential form, and that existential form is only interpretable through exchange (even if we restrict ourselves to notice of a being's internal exchange, what it becomes from moment to moment)? Death persists in a double exchange. A being's internal constitution thrives on this persistent exchange, and that being becomes a subject within an external negotiation. You will notice that we have invested death with a quality we find intractable, consciousness. What a maneuver. We affirm qualities by denying them as existent in one domain, and by placing the highest value upon them in an antithetical domain. All that we seem truly to have determined is that no complex, no process, is of any value in itself.

Our search is, and has been, for a value that transcends our consciousness, that makes our consciousness strange and vulnerable. We can acknowledge, as we have acknowledged, that consciousness means being continually present to oneself.

This acknowledgment does not do away with our vulnerability. If anything, it emphasizes and, if I might put it so, broadens the frame of our vulnerability. We cannot pretend to be in control of our own consciousness. You might see this as absurd. You might argue that consciousness is the one thing within this vital complex that has to be stable. We have to see ourselves as living, and we have to be aware of our approaching death, even if we will come to that point, the moment of death, and find ourselves unable to go beyond that point, to stand outside it as though we were watching a natural process that subtly rearranged our being and set us on the road to a transcendent awareness that involved us but, through its commonality, held us apart. We have, all along, argued that there is no fixed point called death, or perhaps, to be more exact, we should say no fixed point within death.

You can see where our explorations lead us. We find it acceptable to speak of being within life, but find it almost impossible to speak of being within death. I have insisted upon an entanglement to say something sensible about the sensibility death embodies, to do away with analogy in order to uncover the distinctive attributes of the phenomena under scrutiny. We have tried to think within two domains, and to live within them.

You might ask, what is the point of living within death, an absurd proposition? And how does one *live* within death? And where does value reside? If the point of this exercise is to go beyond what we know, what are the terms of our knowing? I realize now that we have come close to that moment Gleick defines in the history of quantum physics, that moment when the profession realized that its relationship to reality had changed, and, as he has put it, no one could assume a single reality and a mind with reasonably clear access to it; experience now had to be interpreted and construed in a way that was always provisional. The Yoruba say, èṣọ̀ l'ayé—life is delicate. My claim is that death shares this delicacy. Do I mean that life and death are provisional, phenomena that might in fact be non-existent? No, they are real enough. They structure a delicate relationship that makes them and their relationship a necessary engagement to a different, transcendent relationship, one we have perhaps encountered but failed to understand. We speak of transcendence, but you should not think this an invitation to walk away from our complex experience, call it reality. In effect, we have tried to establish a complex domain that will transform itself into an instrument capable of structuring a possible realm of experience, one that might have been there as the third who walks beside us.

The Counterfactual Self

Freud's geistige forces cannot be grasped by the senses; they are the movement of air that (as Freud declares) provides the prototype of intellectuality. One has to be open to such an argument, to be able to see that geist derives its name from "a breath of wind."

——— ———

Consider Mudimbe's "étude sémantique," with the analytical, structural, and, one might propose, mathematical temper of this "breath of wind."

——— ———

Concerning that "breath of wind," Bernstein gives animus, spiritus, and the Hebrew ruach (breath).

$$1\text{–}5$$
$$a + (b + c) = (a + b) + c$$

Follow Nadler's design for the tripartite soul, and find there: ruach, the animal soul bound up with animal emotion and human passion, distinct from and intimately related to neshamach, the intellect, subject of higher cognitive functions and, for some rabbinic authorities, inseparable from the body.

*

Have I overlooked Nadler's heresy? Did I even derive these notions from Nadler? Or have I simply followed an appealing notion that I want to turn into a commonplace?

Can we say with Carnes that religion "is the crystallization of religious experience into a structure of words, concepts, artifacts, people, and social relationships"?

*

Within this domain, we encounter the laser that cuts into first facts, no one of which can claim priority.

*

Thinking about religion and religious experience leads to theology, what Carnes calls a purely intellectual discipline. Obviously, religion and religious experience are theology's objects of thought. It must be absurd to insist upon thinking without an object of thought in this case. But what if we were to consider *experiencing* without an object of thought? Must we stay close to thought because the body is involved in this experience? And must we always be cognizant of the body, even when we say that we have "taken leave of the body"?

*

What does the body think, if not itself? For that matter, what does the thought think, if not itself? We could carry on in this round, asserting that experience experiences itself, and carry on to the end of this hermeneutical process until we do not, and cannot, understand the relationships configured by body, experience and thought, effectively doing away with any phenomenological presence.

*

Can we conceive of life as a conceptual system? If we do so, have we constructed that system from thinking, experiencing and talking?

*

How might we take a perturbative approach to the word, conceptual?

The meditative mind might call for a review of our pronouns, those that refer to a state of being. Standing within any particular state of being provokes an uneasiness about all other states you might enter, and will make you question the relationship of states you have taken for granted.

*

6–8

$$a\,(b + c) = (a \cdot b) + (a \cdot c)$$

Who can account for the relational configurations that justify the momentary derivation of the self? The self is only thinkable if we can think incorrectly, be wrong about the world and that state of being to which the world belongs.

Misapprehension presents the self with an opportunity to re-construct the phenomena under regard.

*

To think incorrectly implies, here, that we construct a parallel world to the one we abandon when we think incorrectly, and it is possible that in doing so we enter upon a further misapprehension, and find ourselves standing nowhere to address this parallel world. We must believe that, in this act of perceiving, the self retains its quality.

Consider the perceptive act in which you might enter and need no self, or find that a self is not required until after the fact of misapprehension and, following the logic of that, the recovery of a prehensive determination.

*

If, then, the self finds itself defined by being absent, what would account for its quality, or any attribute that consciousness would reveal? How could the self escape such a dilemma?

*

Where is the flaw? Is the self formally embodied in the thinking of it? Can the self be formally embodied in experience? Can we talk with any precision about a self that remains only a formal possibility in a total conceptual system? We should understand (if we want to think about misapprehension thinking incorrectly about the self) that we cannot avoid thinking about a total conceptual system in which no element within it contributes to its definition. That parallel world would then become the only world.

*

What have we done, standing above this urn? We have made consciousness only a quality of error, or, stated without subterfuge, we have made error the only quality of consciousness. This results from running headlong away from any definition of quality.

*

Let us now acknowledge a drive toward limitation. We appear to have entangled ourselves in the idea of a conceptual system that cannot accommodate the idea of quality because we can only constrain the misapprehension we want to propose and yet cannot get around to a bound understanding of what, if anything, matters.

9–17

$$x\,(a+b) = xa + xb$$

The text exemplifies a misspelling. Nothing should encourage the spirit thinking of thinking to take this significant digression to its heart.

*

How do we spell invention? Let us take a scandalous approach. Apollonius with his hybrid mathematical form may be ποιητός, himself an invention, or a grammarian only feigned. But every geometer signs himself, saving the generic appearances πιστικός, faithful to that misspelling, ποιότης. Why sound the bell for Apollonius at this point? In order to speak, qualis needs an arbitrary segmentation of ποίησις, and perhaps a theory of opaque Hellenistic number.

As with Apollonius, so with our metaphysician—water and the ludic proof remain the functional image of reality. Even this line must change its shape, play within a Dioclesian garden, moving from sunlight to shadow and back again, searching for the significance it will acquire through participation in the body's practice and the textual ambiguity the spirit defines.

*

How do we approach the gúru sọ̀? How should we conceive of the word in the nest, the sheltered enigma? Where would we meet that φύσις τις κοινή ("a certain common nature") grasped αὐτό καθ᾽ αὐτό ("itself by itself") if not in the mythic mathematical ratios, Anaximander's coin, distributed in Djenné?

We are far too comfortable living with our ethical failures and aesthetic compromises. We seem unprepared for the judgment consciousness requires. Perhaps we feel that, because of our talent for improvisation, judgment (a necessary ethical decision) can wait.

*

What does it mean to improvise, when all actual occasions arise as formal event?

*

Improvisation allows for the slow cooking of fundamental ideas.

*

Improvisation encourages the self to be incorrect, to be exploratory.

Why should physicists preen themselves on their hypothetical expertise? Why should they discount the idea of a conceptual system that cannot accommodate the notion of quality?

*

Say that the physicist feels constrained by the misapprehension the self might want to propose, and yet might not get around to a bound understanding of what, if anything, matters.

*

Here we have the lemma of a bound self freely expressing the mathematics of the senses.

What does matter—if our preparation for a significant act becomes a problem? How might we argue for the intuitive mathemata of the self?

*

Nothing follows if one disposes of relation. "The other," Klein tells us, represents the ultimate source of all articulation.

*

"Analysis merely shows the *possibility* of a proof or a construction. A theorem has been 'proved' only when the facts in question have *actually* been 'derived' from the 'given' relations between the 'given' magnitudes. The construction of a figure determined by certain definite conditions has taken place only when this figure has actually been drawn using the magnitudes 'given' with *just these determinate dimensions*. The 'givenness' of which analysis makes use should, by contrast, be understood only as a 'possible givenness.'"

*

No one feels secure enough to propose the self as a given magnitude, or a proportion taken as the construction of an ontological equation. The messiness involved in going from "things better known to things sought" becomes an insurmountable failing, an embarrassment to every calculational attempt to find the self's instrumental indeterminateness. No one has Diophantus's ease with the multiplication of expressions, composed of numbers of different kinds. The self, to return to what threatens to become only a symbolic expression, cannot, under such stringent and confused conditions, measure itself or its own possible magnitude, as measured by an indeterminate relation.

*

What does matter—if our preparation for a significant act becomes a problem? Is every internal improvisation (meaning within the self) significant? How could the self know? What would tell the self how it might act, or how it has already acted? These matters have found expression in other terms, terms that seem only to reconstitute the self. Given such deviance, nothing appears worth arguing except a different understanding of improvisation.

*

Improvisation, we notice, depends upon a superior form of organization. Why then call it improvisation? And why treat the notion as a singular phenomenon and not as the multifaceted phenomena the evidence suggests?

*

We beg nothing if we say that any form of improvisation re-
quires the ideas of subject and object. Some subject intends to
perform some act upon an object, or with an object. We enter
an unusually fertile situation, even if we only attend to the
phrase, with an object.

*

Consider subject and object joined in a process that has to
change radically. Assume that subject and object subsist in a
prior situation. Their improvisatory act begins before the im-
provisation. In accepting this last notion, we seem to have over-
looked a step in our reasoning.

*

Improvisation depends upon an ordered sequence, a hierarchy of event. The notion surfaces so easily we feel it almost a canonical expression that enters as a guide to our deliberations. The analyst faces a proliferation of motive and implication, leading to a deductive, or an inductive, encounter with improvisation.

*

Nothing in the structure of the world should lead to a symbolic calculus that proposes a *"lawfully' ordered course of events."*

*

The analyst might retreat in searching a solution 'in the indeterminate form,' opposing the construction of any equation and thereby casting out the idea, seemingly natural if one considers canonical form, of transformation.

*

Turn for a moment to Cornelius Castoriadis addressing Plato's *Statesman* and informing his seminar that we are obliged to grant that every human subject "has to possess a priori a subjective organization" to deal with what the world offers. Castoriadis speaks of this as a capability on the subject's part.

*

Suppose we speak of the capacity an object might display in being the point of its own objectivity. Can we imagine an objective point where the object might organize itself, establish itself as its own premise without regard to the deductive need of any subject? We must understand that the analyst begs a lot when she proposes that improvisation requires a subject and an object; she finds herself thrashing about to distinguish an active agent with an immutable profile engaged in a mutable transaction.

18–23

$$a + (b + c) = (a + b) + c$$

The problem here might lie in treating subject and object as equivalent terms. Within any context of a total conceptual system, the work gets done by individuals whose grammatical function depends upon difference and participation in a textual practice. And we speak incorrectly when we speak about an agent with an immutable profile. We must mean that a subject functions as a variable within such a context, marking and being marked by the various activity that the context allows; what we say of the subject applies to the object. We cannot think, however, that we have defined subject and object, or have set any constraints upon them.

*

We begin to address the self's spatio-temporal address, only here through indirection.

Hartshorne speaks of Hume's extremism in the characterization that tells us that between successive states of a substance or individual there is no identity, only at most a similarity. Our rhetorician then turns to the problem of Leibniz's parallel (according to our rhetorician) extremism, which tells us that the law of the succession of states in a monad makes the individual completely identical with itself at all times. This might lead to Whitehead's prehension of preceding states, the you-now, I-now final units of reality, the multiplicities of such units—the dispositive self.

*

Shall we face the counterfactual proposition of the dispositive self, not at all a proposition of the dispossessed? Doing so requires an understanding of the spelling and grammar the self involves, without any attempt at making the self linguistically and metaphysically irrelevant. Have we now placed constraints upon our subject and object? Perhaps we might see a primary constraint that paradoxically draws us no further than the surface, meaning, we argue, that the constraint remains purely physical.

*

"I think that Maxwell was rather indifferent to the metaphysical thesis of structure . . . it is philosophers rather than scientists who like to think of the universe as characterized by a deductive structure of laws."

*

A physical constraint upon the self would require no ceding of control of behavior and no consummate definition of the self's domain. The analyst could make do with Carnap's protocol statements as manipulated through logic, and insist that a given linguistic framework thoroughly determines the objects that exist for that framework.

*

What would the analyst understand in this? Orenstein insists that Quine's "Ontological Relativity" recognizes that empiricism does not "uniquely determine which objects are required as the values of our variables," and reminds us of the inscrutability or indeterminacy of reference, making it a question of which ontology to accept.

*

Let us pose a trivial question: What is the number of the self that is physically (externally) constrained?

It does not pay to attend to Hacking on predication, particularly as he leads us through Kant and Frege. Should we believe Kant when he "teaches" that existence is not a predicate? Should we agree with Frege when he says that "being one or more in number is very much like existence—not a predicate, or . . . not a predicate of things"?

*

Hacking reasons that "existence and number are, in their primary usage, concepts that apply to concepts."

*

Have we found the science of the self here? In this awareness, what stands as a transparent response to a given, a function noticed by Hartshorne, that our empiricists would propose as self-evident?

Hacking's fundamental question arises through Kant and Frege, and encourages him to speak of being as only possible or apprehensible through conceptualization.

*

Can we dispense with the theory of meaning? Picture an apprentice who will try his sentences without any attention to referentiality. The apprentice must, we might argue, submit to grammar's ethnic force, or must propose a triple A of repudiation—setting aside all affinities, assessment and adversarial advances—because there is no breath of a perfect syntax and no hint of any subtleties in performance.

*

The body's indeterminacy confuses the self.

Think of a necessary reconstruction that mirrors the body's rallentando, the brief notation only captured by a suspected breath. The question of which ontology to accept surfaces without a determinate order. The self appears imprisoned within the indirection of its spatio-temporal address.

*

Dante, contemplating Paradise, found himself troubled by umbriferi prefazii, shadowing prefaces. Peter Dronke would place these prefaces, these presences, within an already shadowed world, one in which every material presence challenged the awakened soul.

*

We come upon another flaw, a misappropriation of algebraic skills. Can the analyst find a logical form that would make the soul an equivalent self? Think now of what such alchemy requires; think of the alchemist's inability to specify what form the hidden variable would take; think of the catalytic confusion involved in all collatio occulta.

*

Must we acknowledge that invisible realities exist beyond languages' known categories?

*

Can the self subsist beyond category? Can the self persist as a nodal point, a concentrated gathering into a movement definable only by its disappearance?

24–28

$$a(b + c) = (a \cdot b) + (a \cdot c)$$

The metaphysical comedian among us turns to a contemplation of particle physics and quantum mechanics, considers the particularly apt security displayed by the physicists. Physicists so engaged in that defensible collatio occulta share an ability to use material imperfectly understood for the exact measure of something they can (in theory) understand.

*

Karin Knorr Cetina reminds us that particle physics (to take one example) operates within a closed field where the objects within that field stand and must function within a strictly specified world. That world, our analyst insists, is reconstructed from within the boundaries of a complicated multilevel technology of representation.

*

Consider the self a particle—"short-lived, transient, subject to frequent metamorphosis and decay, and always mixed with other components that mask its presence."

*

How would we begin to specify those components that mask the self's presence? Can the metaphysician take what she sees or apprehends at the level of awareness as evidence of a specifiable fluctuation of outer and inner movement, as a mark of a passing phenomenon that promises to embody itself?

*

Lemma: what components of the self do not belong to the self?

*

Lemma: could the soul be a necessary component of the self?

Now the analyst must go forward with excision. If, as Harts-horne asserts, "most of the universe is and must remain quali-tatively mysterious to us," where would the cutting begin? Some grasp of principles of classification appears necessary. Shall we run with Strawson, and insist that this apprehension means that the analyst should have full command of the names of things? Critical thought halts at that threshold. Strawson himself can go no further in his definition of objects than to give us identi-fiabilia, subjects of indispensable first-order predication. The definition seems to turn upon itself when Strawson tells us that these subjects have no individual essences and that proper names for persons (and here the analyst plays a trick of dis-placement) have no individual sense.

*

What has happened to the self? Or to put it another way, why has the analyst pulled away from treating the self as discoverable within the closed field where some form of representation might occur? Think again of the particle's world, the natural objects, the quasi-natural objects (defined by Knorr Cetina as the debris of particles smashed in particle collisions); think again of Knorr Cetina's apt characterization of these objects as "unreal" or "fantasmatic." Recall that these objects are too small to be seen, too fast to be captured, too dangerous to be handled. We find a challenge once again in a collatio occulta.

*

What could matter if the self refuses to submit to an excision? We seem to need the paring of attributes, if not the establishment of attributes. How does one account for an object that will not stand still and that disarmingly dresses itself with components that are themselves in disguise? Think only of the soul, if nothing else, a hidden companion that gives no sign and is not under its own aspect.

*

Could we think of the discovery, the illumination of the self as occurring within a trading zone under constraints at different levels, the local coordination Galison has marked in finite traditions?

*

29–34

$$x(a + b) = xa + xb$$

What is the finite tradition of the self? And, if we could specify all those traditions relevant to a parsing of the soul, or of the self, would that enterprise bring us to understand, or even to delineate the self's domain?

*

Galison speaks of the "social, material and intellectual mortar binding the traditions of experiment, theory and instrumentation." How can the analyst escape the incorrigible abstraction and the counterintuitive absence the self presents?

*

hic et ubi
procul et prope
distat et astat

Can the self ever be ἀντελής? Is there a master whose gift for invention could refashion an abstraction?

*

The body proposes its own fable and the actual existent thing, which we will propose as a sign of itself. Peirce will not submit this phantasm we have conjured to the qualitative austerity of his trichotomy; no alchemist could find the ontological law that would make the self's body coextensive with its quality.

*

Can we imagine a soul's ecliptic where the self and the body disappear?

*

Who, or what, serves the laurel, if there is no suffering, no association with death?

Does it come down to this—the body's ingenuity in capturing a critical moment that has already passed? All resolutions, within this compass, must be deliberate and refashioned as a singular and impersonal irresolution.

*

We cannot know the quality of a "breath of wind."

*

A mischievous analyst sees self and soul as an asymmetric relation. A pernicious analyst sees a triadic ratio, with the body as the only definable material component but one that has no particular status in constructing a person.

*

Does the soul need a person?
Does the self need a person?

Can we speak of an asymptotic freedom that encompasses self and soul? That vision would obviate any triadic ratio, and do away with the body as a necessary ratio.

*

The analyst struggles to find a simple operation, one that would make sense of such indefinable elements. Counting will not work; there exist no logical definitions of signs that do not grow naturally from a formal statement.

*

What analytic truth can the self itself propose, after the introduction of any free variable?

What does the self confront if not its own death? Think of death as a verification of Being, though the desert fathers in Albuquerque do not.

*

Verification, as a term, comes from an extraneous domain, and relies upon its eccentricity in order to reveal the strangeness of Being, yet nothing can verify its domain. What can establish the trading zone in which death finds itself?

*

Nothing on its own can verify. The logic of such a statement leaves us with an undisclosed term—*confirmation.*

What can the analyst discover in this: the abrasiveness of confirmation? The desert fathers in Albuquerque repeat an unassimilated story, argue against the self's confirmation, insisting that no confirmation is necessary to the self's functioning.

*

Looking at a kachina on an otherwise empty desk provokes a quarrel with function, if only with the term's definition.

*

No one can apparently approve of the entangled states, function and confirmation. The mind resists such a designation of stated properties, resisting, above all, the notion that function and confirmation represent states and show themselves as operative within the self's domain.

$$35\text{--}41$$
$$(x + a)(y + b) = x(y + b) + a(y + b)$$
$$= xy + bx + ay + ab$$

Think of the soul's ingenuity, disguising itself as abstraction. Consider again the quantum clover, the "best possible copy of a quantum state," and the necessary control of the propagation velocity of the light carrying an entanglement. Consider again the twin beams and the danger of mistaken measurements engendered by light.

*

Think on this: "The awakening of the soul by contact with beauty, via what modern psychology might style a sublimated erotic impulse, is the only remaining window of opportunity to the perception and reception of true forms by human perceptual apparatus." Has our geographer, here, entered upon a trading zone?

The geographer has measured the distance from Miletus to the western delta of the Nile, and has proposed a summer wind coming from the north, and an ambiguous trading zone among the "inquirers of what is."

*

The mathematikoi in Québec have no sense of humor. Dance there becomes no more than a linguistic gambit, a trick of proportion. The self counts upon the corrupt amplitude that defines the landscape.

*

The akusmata in Mali speak caressing the Spanish vowel.

Wǫlǫ empties this necessary anonymity and ambiguity. Could words go blind before Faro? Could the geographer have mapped the wrong sense? Could a voice appear before the body, and figure the world in the soul and its double?

*

The physiologoi in Hanover insist upon the physis, the true nature of a thing. But the body has no nature to discover.

*

The body cannot be grounded in its origin.

*

The self cannot be grounded in its origin nor in what-is-not, though that might give rise to Curd's predicational monism.

The Yoruba propose Èmǐ for the bare fact of animate existence. The initiate must learn the associative value in the breath, but must always remember that breath is not èmǐ.

*

The apprentice wants to argue for all ungrounded theological systems, for a certain dynamic immobility found among the Bamana, Dogon and Akan.

*

Could the soul find its ethical existence in Zipaquirá, near that wellspring served by death, as Fuentes instructs us? All appears a mathematical necessity that has no regard for numbers.

The initiate sifts the dangerous words: necessity, coming-to-be, one. The analyst struggles to admit the awakening of the soul as a structural component occasioned by beauty.

*

Pythagoras does not understand how, seeking a good rebirth, he has managed to trade away the only impulse that sustains him. He denies any dependence upon a geographer mapping an old ontology; he will not acknowledge any predicational precedent; he will not trouble himself with any prepositional anxiety. Let our friend Mourelatos deny the existential "is."

Can the Yoruba Parmenides sit with the veridical "is"—εἶναι, to be the case, to be true? Should we believe him when he tells us that Die Welt ist alles, was der Fall ist, the definitive and unassailable truths suborned by a translation?

*

What was given value in that ungainly translation of two functions (could we mean soul and self?) in a definable ratio? Which, if we had to choose, would we designate as the independent variable? Where would we place the necessary limit?

*

The Bamana understand the strict composition of ti baw. The analyst insists the Bamana represent the result of such composition. Such a definition argues that the analyst has succumbed to an unrepresentative closure.

Dyibi, taken for darkness, will always submit to the signs' flow.

*

The gem of an Anscombe opens the war notebooks, and finds there a fundamental problem in philosophy: Is there an order in the world a priori, and if so what does it consist in?

*

What happens when the literati gather around the master in a "noisy atmosphere of disharmony and querulousness"? No olive branch there, though the olive will always frame the body. Or should we say that the olive, or the idea of the olive, makes possible a return to blessedness?

42–50

$$a(b + c) = (a \cdot b) + (a \cdot c)$$

Under the license of the *Tractatus*, let us now frame two propositions—one involving blessedness, one involving disharmony. The analyst questions the assertion that any possible proposition will be legitimately constructed, and quarrels with the notion that an assignment of meaning to its constituents is all that the proposition requires.

*

The body can give no adjectival meaning to blessedness, and can offer no propositional solution to its disharmony.

*

Richard Goode, in discussing George Perle, finds in the music an order analogous to tonality, one that is an outgrowth of twelve semitones.

Is the self an object that can only be named? Can we only speak *about* it through its representatives, signs, and never know what *it* is?

*

The analyst searches for an order analogous to the self, the possibility of structure, the possible facts in which it can occur. The order itself cannot appear without revealing the internal relations that determine the properties that govern all constituent facts.

*

Has time taught us to read the master's early text? "Each thing is, as it were, in a space of possible states of affairs. This space I can imagine empty, but I cannot imagine the thing without the space."

Where now could we set the self's space? The self cannot acquiesce in this: "an object's identity is internally related to the possible facts in which it can occur."

*

Think now of the external impulse that searches its internal origin. Think now of the external impulse unaware of an internal origin, or one that denies whatever can be defined as internal.

*

Where is the flaw? The analyst insists it lies in accepting an objective possibility as fact. The self, sheltered by its self-forgetting, finds this argument disingenuous, in danger of a silence that cannot be overcome.

The self dances within a closed field, or so the analyst says. Is it the body that calls our attention to a nodal point we might specify as self? Is it the body's task to remind us of fluctuations of inner and outer movement with regard to umbriferi prefazii, those shadowing prefaces that remind of presences that can never occur but, by some sleight-of-mind or sleight-of-spirit, might define.

*

Our analyst wants the mathematical substance that, in this instance, no one can have. The analyst cannot even be sure that this instant is a substantive event.

Concerning Quine, Orenstein proposes that Quine recognizes two "different sorts" of indeterminacy. The reader becomes attuned to a modest Quine: "the indeterminacy of translation that I long since conjectured, and the indeterminacy of reference that I proved, are indeterminacies in different senses. My earlier use of different words, 'indeterminacy' for the one and 'inscrutability' for the other, may have been wiser."

*

The philosopher prepares his stand: "With Dewey I hold that knowledge, mind, and meaning are part of the same world that they have to do with, and that they are to be studied in the same empirical spirit that animates natural science."

Should the apprentice now understand inscrutability as an indeterminacy of reference, and flow toward a recognition that will soon become troublesome for the counterfactual self?

*

Where does the evasion lie, if Ontological Relativity recognizes empiricism's forbearance, never requiring a strict determination of the values of any variables? How, then, can the empiricist decide upon which ontology to accept?

*

Consider the self an empiricist. This empiricist might find no plausible way to meet those "observational constraints" advanced by Orenstein, might find it in fact onerous to think ontological thoughts at all.

Does the self know inscrutability? Does the self recognize any external constraints, or will it rest content with establishing nothing other than internal constraints? What makes the analyst question the self's ability to deal with the a priori event that every embodied self displays?

*

How outrageous to think of a necessary truth of a variable without value. The analyst vuole spaventare; the analyst wants you to consider emptying the self of value.

*

The analyst finds the self bound in a Plotinian order, confronted by an uneasy concession to an external constraint. In order to see the order, the analyst must reinterpret the offensive Plotinian number.

The self cannot separate from itself. What would emptying, then, accomplish? Speaking of emptying leads into the body's province. And that leads one to think of the body's discipline.

*

Can the self submit to the body's discipline? We come upon two forms of astringent determination, two forms of obeisance to power. The body's material presence contends with qualities the Bamana have attributed to the person in sebaya and nafolo, defining attributes of intellect and fecundity.

*

Who would argue now that the soul stands as the perfect variable?

Cantabrigians seem to have lost their aspect, being now unable
to define the primary properties of substance. Would that now
be a matter of the soul's domain, or the body's usurpation of an
endangered terrain?

*

Has the analyst created his own mistake? Is it necessary for the
analyst to acknowledge an indeterminate empiricist, a pragma-
tist who will refuse the name?

*

We might say that the body comes to rest with a recentered
being. As this motion begins, there appears a practical solution
to a dilemma occasioned by physics. The self, in effect,
disappears.

51–54

$$x(a + b) = xa + xb$$

Can the self truly come to rest without confounding the soul's power and the dilemma occasioned by physics in the body's domain?

*

Cantabrigians will pretend to discover the sameness in observational constraints, contending that only observation sentences impose external constraints upon a system. At the same time, Cantabrigians want a quality of action, or a state, the self finds it impossible to provide.

*

The self must bear up without a body's interpretation, or risk a constraint that endangers its other bearing in the soul. Yet nothing has, as yet, in this account, measured, or even implied, that first primary property.

The analyst has spent too much time in Elis, among philoso-
phers too comfortable with their numbers and veils, too un-
comfortable with repetition and duration, the sight-specific site
of an otherness that disturbs.

*

Nothing here is as cryptic as the skeleton the analyst would
abandon for the durable obscurity the soul recommends.

*

Think carefully of the angular distance between two points seen
from nowhere. What signifying relation can sound that
mutability?

*

Mana, siri ⟶ spirit light,
          distinction

Can we speak of the soul as deixis, a portrayal, an acting out of the body? Can we speak of the body as deixis, an interpretation, a representation of the self? We go from latency to conceivability, to a denotation of form that must always remain submerged, little more than an allusive element in a prescribed figure.

*

Look for the picture in the dance, the pattern of motion that permits no separation, no necessary emptying of value, no variable without its attendant ontology.

*

Something here seems betrayed, or perhaps seems a betrayal. The attentive observer must take the point, make a decision.

You might consider the body a speculative genius and at once a rugged guardian of its own property. It makes contracts within its deme. The analyst argues for a transactional symmetry that relies upon a triadic structure which even the analyst cannot specify.

*

Shall we force, if not persuade, the apprentice to accept what is the case? We can offer no greater choice than this wandering, this "centrifugal ecstasy," a standing out of oneself.

*

The self that would lead the perfectly attentive apprentice into the path of small opaque white beads, perhaps there to encounter the allusive ambiguities of such visible signs, becomes itself an incomplete sign.

55–60

$$(x + a)(y + b) = x(y + b) + a(y + b)$$
$$= xy + bx + ay + ab$$

Those who might argue "what is the case" impose a concern with whatness, essence, not existence. Only these advocates can lift the analyst's required veil, and see there the κρίσις the body refuses.

*

Let us follow the speculative tempering of the body's grasp on its space. All tempering must oppose the self's disjunction.

*

What if the self awakens without the feel of its instrument. But have we taken the measure of that instrument? Can we even speak of an instrumental understanding of the self?

Must we go now into the bush, or down by a hidden river, to gather the ritual reality of an absolute authority? The analyst struggles to establish the self's command in establishing its own design.

*

Think again of those small opaque white beads and an activating force that must remain indivisible.

*

The soul refuses any plausible translation into a visible sign. Upon these grounds, the soul declares its empiricist commitment. How can the analyst persuade us to speak of the soul's construction in observational sentences?

Among the Yoruba all names are complete sentences. The Austrian says that only objects can be named. Shall we propose, then, the body as object, and search the spatial claims upon its identity?

*

The Austrian Yoruba does not want to be clever, does not want to argue with the tacit metaphysics of space, and yet feels obligated to determine the internal relations that govern a counterfactual self.

*

Someone must press the analyst for a clearly proposed notion of place. What motivates this churl, who seems prepared to stir up a quarrel among empiricists whose mathematics resists becoming a logic?

The apprentice steps over his analytic tutor, believing the latter too easily spooked by an Eleatic discontinuity, too easily undone by the accident of identity. Nothing speaks as swiftly to the apprentice's soul as the notion that it thrives upon an impossible constitution that has no grasp upon its space.

*

Have we come to that point where the body has to accept that it must remain incomplete, and always in opposition to a counterfactual self?

*

What counterfactual proposition will allow us to oppose the self's disjunction and the body's speculative tempering? What constraints would help us to spell this triumvirate's theoretical presence or, for that matter, its existence?

Can the soul submit to a distributive law?

*

Could the Austrian construct anything that would make the soul an element of the self? Could he do anything at all to make the self an element of the soul? Where does the decentering begin, if it must begin at all?

*

The analyst does not want to argue with himself about the materiality of starlight. That is why he avoids specifying the body's tactile range. You will, of course, see the greater fear in such evasion—the possibility that the body might find its true measure.

Is it possible to write a sentence, a predicate expression for the self? For the soul? Even for the body?

*

We keep looking for an easy solution for our dilemma. Analogy sends us into an unmerited ecstasy. We fall into a fever of Dantean transformative practice; we keep to our singularities; we eschew the derivation of starlight. Yet we understand that symmetry breaking needs a new particle, some force, or forces, that will not (or cannot) bear the names we have assigned our transactional symmetry—the self, the soul, the body.

$$61-64$$
$$x(a + b) = xa + xb$$

Perhaps, within this world, "there is no quantum world. There is only an abstract quantum physical description."

*

Should we listen to these heretics?

> "I understand now that
> there isn't anything
> to be understood."
> (Freeman Dyson)

> "The more the universe
> seems comprehensible,
> the more it seems pointless."
> (Steven Weinberg)

> "in so far as the propositions
> of mathematics refer to
> reality, they are not certain;
> and as far as they are certain
> they do not refer to reality"
> (Albert Einstein)

The analyst warns against taking advantage of a certain skepticism concerning observable phenomena.

*

Shall we include Lawrence Sklar among the heretics, "Next, there are those doubts about the simple truth of our theories," and these theories, shading into a fundamental theory that "is applicable to systems in the real world only after numerous crucial idealizations have been made," might, in the end, please our Cantabrigians and be canonical among our empiricists.

*

The apprentice still has no answer for starlight, or for the speculative exigencies of a sacramental symmetry.

The apprentice has gone through her commonplace book, looking for a system, or at least the sọ̀: ẹ̀du, the bonne parole, something reflected in a Standard Model, but finds only the silence.

*

Kepler, they tell us, never accepted light's independence; he felt that it could only misrepresent "infinite natural circumstances." But then think now of Alison Cornish reading three verbs in the opening line of *Paradiso* 13: to imagine, to understand, to desire (Augustine's image of the trinity in human beings: memoria, intelligentsia, voluntas).

*

The apprentice now wants to set aside all books, to dress the soul with desire.

The analyst loves the report of the soul's intensional phenom-
enology, the self's imaginative logicism, the body's Lockean
analytic. The analyst would close the book on any star-shaped
understanding, that is, on the empiricism that appeals to the
Cantabrigians.

*

This speculative poet will always relish contradiction. Our la-
tent metaphysician perhaps feels himself between a poetics of
textuality and a poetics of presence, truth—the grammatologi-
cal and pneumatological consciousness defined by Segal. The
apprentice intuits the Mediterranean feel of the propositions,
and repudiates them.

65–68

$a(b + c) = (a \cdot b) + (a \cdot c)$

The analyst does not know how to take a presence that seems comfortable with its obscurity. The analyst gets trapped in a grammatical game, as in this case, gets paralyzed over how to address this presence (as "who," "that," "which"), and becomes thoroughly confused about the phenomenon as an objective or a subjective event. To compound this existential distress, our astute analyst wakes up to the realization that it does not matter which of our existential presences we intend to examine—the obscurity appears built into the bones of a defining proposition.

*

The analyst appeals here to the language's flexibility. The question then becomes—what language?

Should we admit ntu, the Bantu equivalent of "to be"? The recovery we might think we find there might lead to another inescapable trap.

*

Why should the apprentice seem prepared to sit with theologians whose symbol of critical examination, and symbol of wisdom and insight, might owe more to Peirce's qualisign than to any Cartesian methodology?

*

Kagame tells us, proceeding confidently upon a perceived agreement, that ntu is strictly and only a copula, and does not express the notion of existence. Here, we must deny that ntu and being are coextensive.

Has the analyst made a mistake in thinking of our triumvirate as qualities? Must the analyst understand quality, as we reason with Peirce, as a sign? The analyst pretends to understand Peirce's insistence on embodiment with respect to the sign.

*

What consequential act can our analyst propose, if embodiment has nothing to do with quality's character as a sign? Have we lost our Parmenidean grounding, or have we simply come to a node in our grammar where signature and rule have no meaning other than the proscriptive meaning our context assigns?

*

Enérgeia (decomposed as en-acted), lovely word that recalls the doing of a thing.

Imagine now the analyst stirring a quarrel among qualities. What would that accomplish if self, soul and body did not understand that each is the embodiment of a quality, pushing toward a particular silence that not only defines but informs it?

*

Here we must ask, to whom or to what can the self, soul or body be informative? It appears that only our analyst needs to think of our trio as qualities. That seems no more than a desperate measure, a way of opening a bodied field to explore.

*

ἀναπλάσσω, lovely word that recalls the notion of form and invention.

$$69–74$$
$$(x + a)(y + b) = x(y + b) + a(y + b)$$
$$= xy + bx + ay + ab$$

The apprentice does not want to relinquish a failing grasp on the notion the analyst has set in motion. Could we not think of a quality as framing (if not forming) itself, making itself useful, inevitable, indisputable, and being an operative force without having a clear-cut name? You might argue that, under such terms, quality can never realize itself, can never attain substance. Then again, is substance required for the being of a quality?

*

The trio scrambles its attributes, seeking, perhaps, to find some common ground, some definition of space, some common measure that measures a common experience.

We will let Hartshorne speak about experience: "Experience, awareness, is never simply of itself, but is always more or less transparent response to a given."

*

Here, the self enters a creative zone.

"One can mean or intend a mere possibility, but experiencing is never merely intending. It is always a having of a given, and this given cannot be a mere 'claim' that something is actual; it is always an actuality. Nor can it be a mere quality, a 'hyletic datum.' Rather, to intend is to use a *given* qualified actuality as sign of something not effectively given. Nor can the given depend upon the experience. It is always independent."

(Charles Hartshorne, Creative Experiencing)

Could the self think of itself as algebraic, a disciple of one who intends to make the darkness light, the complex, simple? Or could the self adopt another discipline, become a poet working to confound the light, to complicate the simple?

*

The apprentice says the self feels comfortable proceeding into a creative doubt, questioning doubt's value in any creative process. Is it the apprentice, or one of those undocumented mentors, who will insist that the truth must be given a new or no dimension? But why now speak of truth or falsity when the self refuses any resolution?

What does the self desire? A blessedness it cannot have without embodiment, the logical constants drawing it into implication and relation, binding it once again in the notion of truth.

*

The Bamana say kidé sọ̀ sọ̀y, and perhaps that reaches us, or we might only understand the phrase, through the ἐνέργεια of a witness as distant as the self. Perhaps what we have, as we speak the word, comes forth as sọ̀ ódu sẹ̀lẹ—a word sans chemin.

*

Have we created nothingness out of a plausible ratio?

The analyst will insist upon a final relational failure. The counterfactual self can never realize its own and established design.

Bone Documentary ↔ Disappearance

Being in the world. We were made for that predicate. We get caught trying to define a relation that seems capable of only one expression. Yet in our spiteful moments we ridicule anyone who questions the proper form (as we see it) of that relation. Let's not talk of saints or transcendent beings. No one can will the self out of the bone document that never disappears.

We hear of quarrels, sense them within ourselves, prepare for what we must think of as a necessary exile. We become confused. How can anyone accomplish such an exile? Where does one go that is not in the world?

I proceed with two ideas: I am a complex configuration of ideas and this complexity is determinate and accessible.

We live upon what the body knows. How do we go about interrogating the body?

I will treat this body as the insignificant significance that makes questioning it improbable and, as often as attempted, confusing and dangerous. Its functioning needs to be as transparently impeccable as it seems to be to one who will use the body to substantiate a vitality that transcends anything the understanding would make of it.

dǫgǫ sǭ-ne kizę fŭ agubu-le
tagañe, kŭgo dugǫmǫlę

Dans la parole (l'idée) dogon, toutes les choses se manifestent par la pensée; elles ne se connaissent pas (n'existent pas en) elles-mêmes.

Shall we take this as the first disappearance?

Russell tells us that no class can have a limit unless it contains an infinite number of terms.

How can we deal with Quine who, having warily accepted "mere aggregates" as a description of classes, argues for freeing the (must we say, any class?) entities from "any deceptive limit of tangibility"? $\longrightarrow$ Consequence: there is no reason to distinguish class from property. Read: $\chi\varepsilon\gamma$ as χ is a member of class γ

$$\chi\varepsilon\gamma \text{ as } \chi \text{ has property } \gamma$$

Danquah's problem lies in Absolute Experience. Danquah proposes Interminable Being. None of this will touch upon limit, nor will it undeceive the infinite.

τὸν φρονεῖν βροτοὺς ὁδώσαντα τὸν
"πάθει μάθος" θέντα κυρίως ἔχειν

Zeus who set mortals on the road to understanding, who made
"learning by suffering" into an effective law.

The basic problem in seeking to exploit rhythm as a field of force lies in the realization that so much in that field is unavailable to consciousness. Suppose that internalized field has designs of its own.

Can my apprehension of consciousness serve to define what each individual cellular existence contributes to the notion that the body might become a structured consciousness?

Pointless consideration 1: Every cellular existence begins, grows and functions in the same way throughout the body.

Pointless consideration 2: The complex relationship of impulse and decay that maintains a state of consciousness proceeds without a defined relationship.

What might become the propositional function of consciousness? Mathematics and a theory of relation will not help the case.

In spite of an instrumental achievement that allows the definition, tracking and servicing of certain impulses, in spite of our abilities to map their intensional design, we cannot say that we have an entrance into that configurational intent. We find ourselves leaving room for a fuzzy intention. The problem remains one not of explanation but of apprehension, the conscious grasp of a labyrinth of movement that we might take as the cause of such apprehension. The body will not help in this because, in itself, it gives no directions to apprehension's structure and flow.

Can I paraphrase David Wallace with regard to this dilemma? Must I regard the implications and relations surfacing here as physical and causal, not logical?

Pride wants logic. Logic can only resist. Anyone persuaded of the necessity of the body will confront the non-logical impossibility of a prior state of affairs.

Can I now address the first dilemma? Are there physical modalities simpliciter "determined exclusively by those laws we regard as characterizing the invariable natural processes of the physical world"? (David Wallace's phrase)

Many questions arise. We might ask about an understanding that posits an invariable natural process. We can go too far along this skeptical road, but we should find no comfort in adding a prefix to variable.

Second question: What do we do with the determination given by law or, to state the proposition outrageously, can any determination find justification in law?

We cannot escape certain considerations. It often seems possible to step away from our own bodies, in order to make sense of them. We find analogy, in certain respects, far more revelatory when the body recedes into a physical context that becomes, to use Barbour's term, Mach All, that is, becomes a relational body within the universe. We submit everything within the universe to the laws of one particular framework so that we can "read" the structuring events as comprehensible from domain to domain, reading, in effect, the structure of that universe of objects as a consequence of the laws that obtain within it. This means that we make assumptions about origins, growth, evolution, decay and death that guide the ways in which we see relations among all objects within that universe.

We can act "as if," as if the sentience we experience represents the body's gathering conscious impulse that will, given the proper attentiveness, make itself available to some higher consciousness, within the body, that orders these varying impulses into meaningful singularities, events that lead to a language which explains the impulse and its intention.

We think we have arrived at a conception of structure and function simply by submitting objects to investigative techniques that reveal what is obviously there. We respond to the revelatory process of our investigations in ways that suggest an assumption underlying a given assumption: that what we come up with is a singular truth, a truth waiting to be expressed.

What allows me to talk about the tangle of rhythms and coun-terrhythms that proceed, for all I know, to different clocks? Can I say that every cell within the body thoroughly understands the clock of its developmental existence? What if every cellular ex-istence attunes to a variety of clocks?

All irresolutions must be deliberate.

What *did* Goethe say on his deathbed?

Can we believe Menéndez Salmón, follow him into a delibera-
tion found on a Kafka page?

  One word:

    What was the word?

      Nichts
      Null
      Unbedeutendheit
      Nichtigkeit

    What was the word?

      Nada
      Nothing
      Rien
      Niente

Take the word as translation from one deliberation to another
where the word can appear only as function; grasping the func-
tion excludes the deliberation. The Spaniard cannot appeal to
Kafka, nor to the irresolution embodied in a playwright's plot.

The playwright looks for a bothersome grammatical understanding, enters a quarrel with concept.

Anscombe questions the notion that grammatical concepts ("even the most familiar ones like sentence, verb, noun") can stand as plain physical realities. For her, there is no "plain man's world of plain things."

Have I confused function with use? Have I adopted, and then adapted, an unassimilable opposition that leads to a necessary translation? I should mark the disappearance, as the adaptation proceeds, of deliberation. Function can give no *"description under which"* (Anscombe's phrase) that gives us an intentional object. Here, Russell would, I think, encounter a problem with his affable conjunction of logic and mathematics. Did Russell believe in the conjurational event that led him to assert the disappearance of "1" and "2," and to insist upon an analysis that one could apply to any arithmetical proposition? Should we really read classes as "merely symbolic or linguistic conveniences"?

Could we now say that we have an argument in heaven? Wittgenstein: "Formal concepts cannot, in fact, be represented by means of a function, as concepts proper can." Can we have legitimate notions of universal fact and logical form? Can an ontological disappearance in Kafka account for a narrative force?

"All this that is temporall, is but a caterpillar got into one corner of my garden, but a milldew fallen upon one acre of my Corne; The body of all, the substance of all is safe, as long as the sould is safe."

Poets tell of the memory in light.

Who has the latest report?

Lightfoils

nanoscale glass rods designed to fly on a ray of light,
propelled (like solar sails) by pressure of photons,
unlike solar sails they bend light giving controlled
lift like airplane wings

In algebra of logic under class system
>> 1 = All   / 1 = True
>> 0 = Nothing / 0 = False

In Boole's algebra X is true
>> becomes $X = 1$ X is false becomes $X = 0$
>> given law $X = 0$ or $X = 1$

Repetitive lesson: Given any condition, there is an object (i.e., class) whose members are all and only those entities that meet the condition.

Repetitive correction: (1) The transient particulars, (2) Coherent unquantifiable independence.

We must remember that Russell says "symbols for classes like those for descriptions, are, in our system, incomplete symbols . . ."

Repetitive lesson, signature A

The poet struggles to raise to recognition a recurrent rhythm at the moment of its realization; a causis principally outside any system of concept; all that is intelligible if treacherously divisible.

Three definitions of rhythm:

(1) succession of phenomena which are produced at intervals, either constant or variable, but regulated by law

(Francis Warrain)

(2) perceived periodicity—It acts to the extent to which such a periodicity alters in us the habitual flow of time . . .

(Pius Servien)

(3) property of a succession of events which produces on the mind of the observer the impression of a proportion between the duration of the different events or groups of events of which the succession is composed

(Professor Sonnenschein)

The mathematician tunes his flute at twilight, an interpretation flowing from kalathos. The logician accepts the grammatical mischief in the performance. There arises something in which the notion of existence is not necessarily present.

Count the recent and perpetual disappearance:
>law,
>the flow of time,
>proportion,

all burnished by succession.

Certain misreadings appear:
>law,
>the flow of time,
>proportion,

all buried by succession.

Leucippus and Democritus tell us that matter forms no continuum; it consists of eternal, invariant, impenetrably hard, homogeneous parts moving inertially in a void.

These atoms differ in geometrical and mechanical properties. Must the poet now understand how the world of appearances arises by collision and conglomeration?

First perplexity: the probability of being in a given element of space.

Second perplexity: the emission or absorption of radiation, the energy from orbit to orbit = hv.

Speak of movement within the house, the ritual exactitude in the Great Mask's realism.

Ancient measures no longer serve.

To begin a refutation of the Great Mask's realism, the observant ritualist must construct a peculiar notion of a quantized angular momentum.

Can we think of "atomism" as a research program within the ritual process? First problem: any ritual hypothesis challenges any attempt at explanation—crudely put, what is equal to what?

Is there within the ritual process a kinetic ratio to orbital frequency?

Consider invariants as explanans.

The Dogon express continuity between individuals outside normal rules of descent. Pure or impure status is a ritual classification defined by obligations, prohibitions, the right to assume certain ritual offices.

Return to the ratio of kinetic energy and orbital frequency as an abstract image exploitable in social organizational matters, the realistic world of theoretical relationships, the domain of a Great Mask established by and in command of its own contradictions.

An imposed notion: The commonplace will go unnoticed until theory places it in need of explanation.

We must take Mondrian's "rapport" as ratio, proportion. Connection does not capture the word. In ratio/proportion Mondrian finds his place among the Greek geometers, Russell, Peirce, Einstein, the Dogon and Bamana ritualists.

"... je dis que le rapport est la chose principale" (Mondrian)

First node: "Le rapport primordial, c'est-à-dire l'angle droit, est certes en soi déjà une réalité vivante, mais elle ne devient telle plastiquement que par la relativité, c'est-à-dire par la multiplicité des rapports." (Mondrian)

Could we make a litany of multiplicities, arising for example among the offices Binu, Lébé, Wagem, Awa?

Could we establish the emission or absorption of energy from orbit to orbit among these offices?

Do we have a way of marking all ration and proportion without falling into contradiction?

gá ⟶ the ficus of consecration

gà ⟶ introduces opposition, complication

   (múy marráy, mais je me suis trompé)

Foundational notion (extensional):
the dialectic of deliberation with regard to the word

When something falls under a formal concept as one of its objects, this cannot be expressed by means of a proposition. Instead it is shown in the very sign for this object. (A name shows that it signifies an object, a sign for a number that it signifies a number, etc.)
Formal concepts cannot, in fact, be represented by means of a function, as concepts proper can. (Wittgenstein, *TLP* 4.126)

Necessary translation:
dǫgǫ sǭ-ne kizę fū azubu-le tagaṁe, kūgo dugǫmǫle
Necessary scholion:
"toutes les choses se manifestent par la pensée; elles ne se connaissent pas (n'existent pas en) elles-mêmes" (Griaule & Dieterlen)

Every variable is the sign for a formal concept. For every variable represents a constant form that all its values possess, and this can be regarded as a formal property of those values. (*TLP* 4.1272)

It is nonsensical to speak of the *total number of objects*.

The same applies to the words 'complex,' 'fact,' 'function,' 'number,' etc.

They all signify formal concepts, and are represented in conceptual notation by variables, not by functions or classes (as Frege and Russell believed). (*TLP* 4.1272)

The astringent classification finds pertinent value and efficacy
in the symbol:

no duna sọ tuma kugo von
[c'est le symbole qui seul est essentiel]

Wittgensteinian puzzle: une sophie, un ensemble ordonné →
22 categories, 12 elements (264) each one head of a list of 22 pair
11,616 signs → the mathematical insinuation of a variable system
sọ: váduru, the extended word, the final detail of abstraction.

Two ways to approach an analytic truth might propose another dialectic of deliberation if and only if X = X, or no tautological sentence appears.

Can we speak of the Great Mask's analytic truth? What would allow a necessary translation?

Only the initiate can rewrite the ceremony. Frege's ᶜᴾLogic leads to a critical mistrust among those for whom the Mask has become its own variable. Why speak of the "linear unfolding of calendar time," of the impossible fulfillment of a noetic space of realization?

The ritualist and the Great Mask do not, cannot, without contradiction, participate in the same configuration of time. Might we speak, as Claude Calame does, of "a semiotic putting-into-form"? This semiotic gap would reveal the difficulty in the ἔτι καί νῦν of all ritual performance.

We must allow Eboussi-Boulaga's notion of the dynamic nature of being, and the logical priority of existence he contends Tempels must presuppose.

The poetic investment embodied in the ritualist opens a methodology that the Mask, in order to be true to itself, must refuse. Calame calls putting-into-form a fabrication, something lying between prefiguration and configuration, transforming every trace into an index (call it, as Calame suggests, a document) requiring reading and interpretation.

Could we now find the correspondence rules of the Mask's performance, apart from the protocol sentence, the observational language that grounds the cosmological and ideological? Placed within the context of the ritual, itself placed within an existential, limited state, can our metatheorist uncover the nested word (the gúru sǫ) in a new formal system? Is such a formal system necessary?

Read your *Principia* ⟶ def. of an elementary function of an individual. The definition proceeds: Given any elementary proposition that contains a part of which an individual *a* is constituent, other propositions can be obtained by replacing *a* by other individuals in succession; this will give an assemblage of elementary propositions.

May we read the Mask as the original proposition φa, and put the variable x in place of *a*, giving φx? One can see a given context (involving that existential and limited state) in which φx is a function of which the argument is x and the values are elementary propositions.

We have learned that, within our existential and limited state, the essential use of øx is to collect a certain set of propositions, all those that are its values with different arguments.

This argument continues in acknowledging that "The essential use of a variable is to pick out a certain assemblage of elementary propositions, and enable us to assert that all members of this assemblage are true, or that at least one member is true."

A troubling question: Can Peano's notion that mathematics functions as a grammar of signs, with the single requirement being the explicit revelation of the codi, tell us much about mathematics, grammar or signs?

"A signification is always distributed through the language of a situation, the language of established and transmitted knowledges. A nomination . . . emerges from the . . . inability of signification to *fix* an event. . . . A nomination is a 'poetic' invention, a new signifier, which affixes to language that for which nothing can prepare it." (Peano)

Could we say that the Great Mask must submit to a set of rules of signification, and understand those rules as the start of a fundamental process that serves to fix an event that seems already established and already prepared within a language of irreconcilable signifiers? Can the Mask, within this context, invent anything?

Have we now introduced a paradox, one that will remain shadowed by Russell's Paradox? Would it help to follow Zermelo's reasoning about that paradox? We find ourselves ready for that contest. The argument leads to this formulation: to admit the existence of a set of all sets that do not belong to themselves undermines deductive language by introducing formal contradiction (that is, the equivalence of a proposition and its negation).

The slippery logic of this Mask concerns us now. Does the Great Mask belong to itself, and is it involved in a signification that can, within any singularly specific context, fix an event which relies upon its ability to perform as a transformative event?

Peter Galison requires us to think about the material culture of microphysics. We must consider the tools on the bench, the methods of calculation, and the roles of technicians, engineers, colleagues, and students. Ivan Van Sertima has asked us to think about the material culture of the phenomenon we call Africa, discontent with the way that the concrete material presence of the continent and its peoples has turned into an airy disquisition on psychic aberrations and inexpressible aspirations that need no material foundation.

Constraining dilemma: How to address the matter of material, as a preliminary form of "thinking about."

Can we define the material culture of the ritual ("the bush")? Can we take those practices and set whatever we define as relevant to their construction and set them against experimental practices?

Axiomatic difficulties: (a) the notion of life as a construction, (b) the notion of the origin of such construction as it leads into an understanding of matter, (c) the difficulty of separating matter from the idea of it entertained by those involved in it, if such a separation can even be critically sustained, and with this (d) the shadow of theoretical propositions.

Grating presupposition: What here is a presupposition?

Galison seems to have set us in another domain where empirical knowledge, which seems to be an a priori understanding within his defined material culture, stands as a challenge, even an offense, to the ritual archivist.

Can we speak of a trading zone? Can we make use of a notion we find hard to give up?

Galison → mimetic images "purport to preserve the form of things as they occur in the world" → the logic tradition, those electronic counters coupled in electronic logic circuits make statistical arguments for the existence of a particle or its effect → Galison says the logical tradition preserves a logical relation among events, and calls this a homologous representation.

We might begin again dissident relations with Galison's two traditions. Can we speak of an image and a logic tradition the ritual archivist might honor? To be blunt, can we use these ideas, methodologically, to uncover the ground of ritual practice as it occurs within any particular domain, and will the methodology the ideas encourage sustain a relevant critique of that domain?

You must notice the primary presupposition at work here—the ritual practitioner operates or, better stated, performs an inquiry into the group's practice, based on theory.

Scandalous proposal: The Great Mask embodies an all-encompassing theory, and the attributes of that theory might look like the experimental theory operative in Galison's two traditions.

The trading zone might, according to Galison, look like this:
        experiment ↔ experimentalist's theory ↔ theorist's
        phenomenology ↔ theory
the image tradition of photographic practices (aiming at non-interventionist objectivity) produces homomorphic representations of nature, the logic tradition of electronic practices (aiming at manipulative persuasion) produces homologous representations / Galison's wordless pidgin.

We face an aporia. Can there be a parallel exhibition, or an exhibition sui generis, of an image tradition within the ritual domain? How can we speak of such a tradition when the goal of ritual performance is persuasion?

Persuasion within the ritual domain needs a new definition. Underlying every event the primary impulse for setting it in motion we must understand as discovery. All we can do about that notion, to bring an analytic balance to our perceived parallel, would require a complication (that is, making it complex) of the term non-interventionist.

Those who would denigrate the Great Mask's field as an area where discovery can occur will fasten upon what they perceive as the impossibility of objectivity within that domain.

Can we remove the Great Mask from the image tradition? Would doing so throw the Mask completely into our defined logic tradition?

Does any of this mean that we have to see the Great Mask as standing under experimental law, with all the attendant associations of an established empiricism?

First node/   Can we have two empiricisms?

Second node/   Is there, as Nagel suggests, an experimental law with a "life of its own, not contingent on continued life of any particular theory"?

Third node/   Can the Great Mask submit to experimental law and yet remain, as we have argued, the foundation of an experimental theory that owes nothing to Galison's image tradition and yet remain a decidable and necessary critical tool?

We must listen to Giovanni Levi, [All] social action appears the result of an individual's constant negotiation, manipulation, choices and decisions in the face of a normative reality—a pervasive reality that nevertheless allows for personal interpretations of freedoms. We should note that Levi insists this kind of historical inquiry "is not concerned with the interpretations of meanings but rather with defining the ambiguities of the symbolic world, the plurality of possible interpretations of it and the struggle which takes place over symbolic as much as over material resources."

Galison, whom we have given a fundamental critical role at this stage of our inquiry, accepts Levi's formulation to help in talking about a history of laboratory culture and its constraints.

The critical initiate wants to establish that the material, and symbolic, culture of the Great Mask is under similar constraints. It does no good to see the performative practices of that culture as leading to an irremediably static social world, one in which no intellectual or affective exchange can occur, one that has effectively closed itself to the world that its own constraints force it to see as in constant motion.

What is the disappearance? A substantive bone documentary, free of error.

A Material Emptiness
or
Entanglement as (a) Decidable Aesthetic Form

We might start with a magnolia tree in twilight sun. Jean-Luc Nancy finds himself astonished by the tree's whiteness, an egg whiteness that can only hold a trace of light, only a Dogon clarity. Autrefois, Nancy traveled a broken path to a sacred wood, and had brought another tree's mark from a darker wood into this vestigial world of magnolia traces and hollows.

*

We speak now of a logical negation of gravitational law. The woman at the magnolia lit by a paradox does not argue with the light's origin or the distinction the lumen proposes at the wood's edge. The egg in the tree's hollow reminds the woman of that first abstraction and the safeguarded token that mends an illuminated thing.

*

The first flaw in this equation comes with a mistaken entanglement producing a light's trace and an egg's color, and the assumption that leads to a distinction of light and lumen. Could our Augustinian woman at the magnolia have already captured an actuality that seems a village habitation? Call it a spirit's delegation that must be withdrawn or redrawn, or call it ọmọ's design within púru.

*

Imagination has given the dichter licence to place a child's bundled body in the magnolia tree hollow, but no didascalian aspirant will ever approve such sanction. The mother has slipped away, and has become an unsuspected subversion.

The magnolia now defines its activity, if not its place. It seems to have no concern with any river, or with any tidal limits. Nothing will get done here by rain falling on the outer slope of an encircling ridge. The dichter might not speak of κράσις, or of σχήματα, notions with an enviable relation to number, even though light in the magnolia raises the perplexity of a child "dormido en la cuna de bronce."

↓

Again, the language of absence. Juan Carlos Bösendorfer taught me that phrase, and gave me the eye for Mizquitl, Póchotl, Ahuéhuetl, the memory of steppes, the Valle de México, the tropics.

*

We must write our third page as a generative rhythm, go beyond all arbitrary pulse so that our count never falters. For the moment, the magnolia's empirical world sustains us. Bösendorfer might say it only offers a fixed notation for the various bodies gathered within it, and these are limiting cases dependent upon memory. Can we then justify our insistence upon a protean material existence? We bury ourselves in error. Only the illegible one among us has a name.

*

No one can mistake the name of the sacred wood—kọmọ tú. But the name refers us once again to place, and the physicists have defined place as a position in initial data space.

So we must set about finding the complex experience about which we can talk. We feel emboldened by Galison and his sharply furnished domains, congenial neighbors all too willing to follow rules, though the rules might everywhere lead to failure.

*

The cantankerous poet wakes to a summer morning and finds the music in "Bulb after Bulb, in silver rolled." If you go there, you might encounter Budick's argument with Bloom, a subtle proposition that arms the lineal experience of the sublime with the repetition of resistance.

Must we acknowledge a pure and static state that precedes all creation? Must we admit a lux sui generis, the intellect's own natural power to know? Where will the untutored physicist look for that first authority? An initiate knows námaraká, force; decomposes that force—ná (mother) mara (authority, possession) ká (superior force). The first understanding surfaces from that first authority. Do we see that first authority as a movement from "outside"? We must mind our distinctions, and not enlist our Scotus quia est.

*

pùru (impurity)   ọ̀mọ (living)

This proposition is necessary.

Some will see an aesthetic fraudulence already surfacing. A scribe proposes a Canadian pianist sitting down to a Bösendorfer, and our own true Bösendorfer does not expect to bind the pianist in the magnolia tree's absorbing light. The scribe will, of course, remain unsatisfied, sensing at this level an intimate discord within himself.

*

But let us suppose a self-consistent rhythm that might "Split the Lark," and open a range of energies that cannot be contained in Zurich or its resonant air.

*

Shall we give in to Popper? We shall not give in to Popper.

Think of our barrio associates in Santa Fe who might contest even those "mechanical interactions based on the (relative) impenetrability of solids," or who might go mad with the dispute of languages.

*

We must always consider a melodic possibility in our narrative. We then would have to think of a compositional strength denied to it. How can we determine the limits of that "single form," perhaps a misunderstanding of motion, or a miscomprehension of Manchester's "Now"?

*

We see now that we might have stepped away from an invigorating notion embodied in memory or imagination, out of fear for a body's corrupt perception.

Our advocate seems to have learned a trick. She instructs us to pay attention to these life-giving modal operators. Shall we call them signs, even though that would start our investigation on the wrong foot? Shall we look for an inverse function?

*

200 SOUL AND SUBSTANCE

Bösendorfer proposes a possibility in El Cafeto's survival. Placement becomes a problem—Enríquez, Zaragoza, Úrsulo Galván, something out of Xalapeños Ilustres. The advocate feels no need to speak about El Fayum's necessity.

*

Find the labyrinth that leads to Pino Suárez and Pitol's Peruvian monastery, but that will not mitigate El Cafeto's displacement. Nor will it sound a Monkish hymn to distance.

So what do we have? A scholarly address in Cambridge. A misspelling in a village mosque in Mali. We could also find ourselves confronted by Mormon missionaries in Chaco Canyon, on our way to the rectangular citadel of Pueblo Pintado.

*

It will take a moment to make this transition, to get around the monastic moment of prayer. Someone has said that this sentence begins with rivers, posing an unanswerable question: how to distinguish *was* from *is not*.

*

Could Ungaretti remember more than pain and devastation on the Emerald Beauty? Or could he turn his attention to Alexandria, a possible solution to *was* and *is not*?

Let us establish all redness as a blue halo of a distant galaxy, one that opens an oceanic path. All oceanic galaxies appear as texts; we might submit them to the competence of our modal operators.

*

The task becomes finding less entropy, more homogeneity and order.

*

Caroline Bynum would never begin with Bernard and his prescriptive allegiance to the self and the coexistence of radical opposites—the body and the soul. Shall we start with rivers or the "verdant bough of the glaucous olive tree"?

*

Consider this: "The sum total of existence is always increasing and it is this which gives the time series a sense as well as an order."

*

206 SOUL AND SUBSTANCE

Can we hear Badiou's unfinished assertion, "Number is coextensive with"? The statement seems a challenge to Eboussi-Boulaga/Mulago and their notion that ntu and being are not coextensive. The silent voice here is Dogon, the number, one, proposed as disorder, incompleteness.

*

We approach the dangers embodied in infinity.

*

A philosopher might begin by proposing that "every well-defined series of terms must have a last term," and continues (if insistent), "creating this last term and calling it infinity."

"The problem of infinity . . . is not properly a quantitative problem, but rather one concerning order."

*

Strophe → antistrophe → epode

*

"Infinity is that which cannot be traversed; it indicates the passage to the limit, the movement of transcending, of going beyond, of overcoming and nullifying the here-and-now of the finite."

*

Why introduce Èṣu Èlegba as a generating symbol, or struggle
with sunsum, the Akan postulate of the individual?

*

Strophe → antistrophe → epode

We might discover a balance in the number two, a geometrical capacity in the number three, or a fertile capacity in the number four. But at this point we cannot accept the challenge of the "predicational is," or insist upon the possibility of being necessary.

*

The examination of number begins in the transfer of goods in marriage, in maturation, and in death, perhaps in the perfect understanding of submission.

*

Why should Curd propose the three Parmenidean monisms—material, numerical, predicational?

*

Could we now introduce a Kantian argument from composition, and there look for a hidden proposal in Parmenides?

The apprentice has bound herself to a fleeting notion, only partially revealed, only weakly defended, of a manifold and changing world that cannot be derived from a single homogeneous substance. Where does the contradiction lie?

*

We come upon an expanding problem of entanglement. Having spoken of a logical negation of gravitational law, we find our philosophy flummoxed by the idea of negation. Addressing entanglement leads to no definition of substance.

*

Does the hidden proposal lie in Parmenides' predicational unity, or in the "word-centered Dogon function ascribed to Yurugu"?

The apprentice faces a paradox. At every ontological level the simultaneity of opposites, A and not-A, must be contradictory.

*

We should reserve such deixis for the magnolia tree's absorbing light and the egg cradled in its hollow.

*

Think of this in mathematical terms: the algebraic variable that disturbs Rotman, the way a Pascalian theology absorbs all potential and actual infinity.

*

Our apprentice suffers through a misapprehension—a being with no boundaries, no negation, notions that might lead to an elemental failing *in* number, if not *of* number.

*

Why linger now with negation? Should our advocate parade the proposal of entanglement? Can we have entanglement without negation?

*

Can we speak of an axiomatic system that will never admit contradiction? Have we uncovered a deeper contradiction, a necessary contradiction that gives value to a necessary absence? And why should we, like Leibniz, tie contradiction to negation?

*

Our advocate tries to go around a damaged spot in the road, trying to move from interpretation to restructuring. We have already found a central problem with proposing a generating symbol.

*

Nothing says go forward with that deixis. We might even read the limits to being (or, more precisely, the notion of being without), in Leibniz.

*

Here we need to take advantage of Mark Wilson's idea of façades, of that "efficient linguistic engineering," in which the fracturing of descriptive tasks creates a place to exploit "localized opportunities," as Wilson suggests, meaning that we should look, not for negation, but for complementarity.

*

Has the apprentice misread Wilson's fracturing as a point of entry? And will she insist that the point of entry opens to a predicational unity, a metaphysical atom?

*

Why should we believe Cusanus who tells us all he thinks we need to know about change? Our younger advocate has been at school with Segal, and has derived—or, more properly, has constructed—a reading counter to a text she feels too surrounded by divinity, too willing to abandon precise relations among bodies. She will claim that we need the exact measure of the dance, even as it escapes our sight.

*

Could Wilson's quilt-work assemblies lead to an internal defini-tion of difference, or a qualitative change beyond the reach of Leibniz's a posteriori proof of contingency?

*

The apprentice grows cold thinking of the qualitative necessity of being, and of the argument Parmenides should not make to establish his predicational is.

*

There remains the perlocutionary act.

*

There remains Prigogine's idea of a non-equilibrium source of order, some will say, derived from the Ionian restless play of warring forces.

*

Shall we uncover those primitive ideas in Russellian epistemology: 0 and 1? Notions that impose an unarguable recognition, according to a plangent logic.

*

We must slip away from that soul that proposes Logoi as noetic completeness, and avoid all quarrel with immediacy.

Does Manchester attribute too much to Plotinean invention in ἐχρόνωσεν? But how attractive to think of the soul falling from eternity into time because of her "will to *originate* and to *be* of herself, to be self-constituted."

*

Shall we do our beads with "order" again?

*

Concerning order, an ordinal element consists of three terms: a, b, c, with b between, and a relation of a to b, b to c. The logician tells us we can consider an ordinal element of four terms: a, b, c, d, with a and c separated by b and d. This proposal quickly gives rise to asymmetrical relations. The apprentice wants to search for a limit.

*

Nothing will here propose a linguistic ingenuity set to solve a problem with succession. Has this now become a mathematical history?

*

No one will now permit the unsuspected subversion of the mother's body, or the lumen's unsuspected subversion of the mother's body.

*

"although two terms alone cannot have an order, we must not assume that order is possible except where there are relations between two terms."

*

We must always find a worrisome mode in the magnolia tree's absorbing light.

*

"But the formulation we are considering concerns not the measurement of time but its nature 'in itself,' with respect to which it is called 'duration.' On this level, time is involved not in the motions of sensible things, but in their being, as it is subject to motion."

*

"The space in which a melody moves . . ."

*

Does our apprentice recognize an order presented in sequence?
Does our apprentice have a feel for music?

*

"There is a prima facie case for the proposition that arithmetic is no less a model for the structure of time as it governs actual or actualizable process than geometry is a model for empirically presented extension in space."

Can we assume the substantive progression of space within the body?

*

Can we assume the structuring, or restructuring, of space within the body and the mathematical exigency of unrecorded, and therefore unresolved, space?

*

Engelbert Mveng would argue an objective realism shading into a second term, a moment of abstraction. Though he proposes an essential line that appears as a generative operation, he might feel himself defined by paradigm and a paradox.

*

Eboussi-Boulaga finds his paradox among the Greeks. Our apprentice might challenge the notion of being's stability contending with an Aristotelian dynamism.

*

Manchester will never consent to the conceptual light of the magnolia tree, yet he will insist upon light as a substance traversing physical space, and insist, too, upon information as an attribute of light.

*

But we must wait upon our philosopher, who will return us to the paradoxical structure that Goldschmidt defines, an "element-form," a sensible phenomenon "re-cognized and produced by an operation."

*

The paradigm here has perhaps faded. The mathematicians want no universal infinite space. Mveng will have to define a thematic movement to rescue his design. Soyinka stands apart, marking his fourth stage.

*

So the body of one takes place as a fall into number.

*

We have spoken of a being with no boundaries. We must re-
member, however, Mark Wilson with his patches and bound-
aries. He will insist, with Nishiura, on the salutary information
concentrated on the perimeter, a notion that would seem to
caution the body about its limits, or to return the body to the
necessary domain of limit.

*

Eboussi-Boulaga and Moulago must deny that fall into number,
yet find no solace in the Kantian argument from composition.
Holden offers them no help in the 'absolutely simple funda-
mental parts,' those metaphysical atoms.

*

Bösendorfer would now ask our apprentice to define an unruly state of being, or to give in to a thorough dis-closure.

*

The apprentice refuses an exhibition that would lead number into the idea of construction. Only there would she find a troubling incoherence, a self-contradiction in the language.

*

"Sometimes words are willing to follow almost any excuse to conquer new territories of application."

*

The magnolia tree's impulse to alter its physical correlates threatens to undo the light, or to send the lumen searching a diagrammatic representation.

Netz has opened a disturbing consideration of Greek geometri-
cal propositions. Reading carefully, we will find no universal
infinite space.

*

How should we accommodate this: "Greek geometry is the
study of spatial action not of visual representation"?

*

Could we have forgotten that egg in the tree's hollow? Could
we forget a bundled body that represents nothing, but exists as
itself?

*

What properties here would the mathematician trade, and with whom or what would she trade them?

Think again of that "particular geometrical configuration"—the magnolia tree, the twilight sun, the egg, the child's body—as "local qualitative features of spatial figures." Will this lead to a system of order? What element would establish it?

*

The magnolia tree's temperature leads us to a consideration of the sun's orbit and luminosity. Lightyears envelop the magnolia and the sun, the distance between a postulated existence and a postulant, the differential of a grammatical and a geometrical configuration.

*

Though our apprentice might only confound cardinal and ordinal, she might return us to a salutary Netzian insight concerning paradigm.

*

Shall we read Cohen and Kopytoff through Amselle? There we shall learn the notion of center-periphery relationships which might act as matrices for political formations. Will the advocate speak again of paradigm, exploring the terms παραδείγματος, γένεσις? Someone will have to contest this "placing alongside," "this conjoining," argue that no linguistic ingenuity can justify the deixis, showing and exposing.

*

Remember the point: "the paradigm is never already given but generated and produced."

*

The Scotus challenge remains. The authentic referent of a simple concept does not represent an external object but the cognitive content of the concept itself.

244 SOUL AND SUBSTANCE

We work hard to establish such flexible boundaries. We might even wish for the radiant energy from four bright central stars to excite a separate measure.

*

What becomes the first term in the general law of Bamoun esthetic creation?

*

We pretend now to understand that all progression in aesthetic order grows from terms that can only submit to a requisite ordinality.

*

We seem to have arrived at a source of order that must originate "une nouvelle idée, une nouvelle apparence des choses."

The poets among us must watch ourselves reading these unwritten, yet scrupulous texts. We have to guard against a buoyant resonance that might lead us into the buoyant bubble of what Wilson would call property dragging.

*

How easy to go beyond significance with this: Das Wirkliche ist uns nicht gegeben, sondern aufgegeben (nach Art eines Rätsels), or as Fine translates it and calls it Einstein's debt to Kant: The real is not given to us, but put to us by way of a riddle.

*

The philosopher wants to put a halter on a supposed Einsteinian "natural holism." So will not here propose the conjunction of this paradigm and the one that set us to property dragging.

Property dragging does not frighten our apprentice. A Wilsonian, she finds nothing odd in thinking of a Bösendorfer who can inhabit the wood, wires, ivory and felt of a Bösendorfer.

*

Shall we call these indefinables, which require no more than simple recognition and the circumspection of a generative method?

*

Could we now insist on no need for a separate measure against which to test a simple concept for truth or falsity?

Think on this fundamental logical fact Russell proposes:
>   where aRb does not imply bRa,
>   there is another relation, related
>   to R, which must hold between
>   b and a . . . that is, a relation
>   Ř such that aRb implies
>   bRa; and bŘa implies
>   aRb.

*

What does our mathematician here propose? We see that "the relation of R to Ř is a difference of sense."

*

We must see this relation as one-to-one, symmetrical, and in-transitive. N.B. Russell argues that the existence of this relation is the source of series, of the distinction of signs, and the greater part of mathematics.

Have we come very far toward defining the elemental order of any geometrical configuration that any body might expose?

*

The poets never understand the complications in these converse relations. They dance around what Russell must define as a synthetic incompatibility.

*

The poets might press against their own incomprehension, and not know what lies buried, or perhaps lies apparent, in this:
"The incompatibility consists in the fact that two terms which are thus incompatible cannot coexist in the same spatio-temporal place, or cannot be predicates of the same existent, or, more generally, cannot both enter into true propositions of a certain form . . ."

*

It seems that we have skated past the moment of abstraction, the second term (according to Mveng) in the Bamoun esthetic, and have failed to grasp an object's essential line, and thus the making of an esthetic sign.

*

How far can we treat the bodies we have conjured as conjugates? How far can we exploit a Wilsonian enlargement of linguistic application, without falling into a tropospheric complacency?

*

Our apprentice stands ready to alert us to an expanding problem that threatens to make any definition of substance and of material bodies suspect.

We struggle not to give in to despair, as Bösendorfer might define it, or as our apprentice would pose that problem for further analysis. This means we must not turn to that generating symbol, Èṣu Èlegba.

*

How could Kant avoid the Akan postulate, sunsum, or escape the word-centered function in Yurugu? And must we, battling our own apprentice, argue against any ontological derivation in these functions?

*

Rotman would deny us the Pascalian theology involved in such potential and actual infinity, and scoff at any three-place relation that seems to have surfaced here.

We think we have found an ally in Holden when he challenges the claim that composition is a contingent relation, and assures us that all composition can be abolished.

*

The apprentice excoriates our imprecision; she wants to return us to the fourth stage of the Bamoun esthetic, as revealed by Mveng, a composition, a synthesis that structures an objective realism.

*

You might hear another voice now calling into question the notion of an objective realism.

*

"Physics is an attempt conceptually to grasp reality as it is thought independently of its being observed. In this sense one speaks of 'physical reality.'"

What can our apprentice make of this: "It is basic for physics that one assumes a real world existing independently from any act of perception. But this we do not *know*. We take it only as a programme in our scientific endeavors. This programme is, of course, prescientific and our ordinary language is already based on it."

*

But who now has said that causal connections exist only as features of theoretical constructs?

*

Can we count upon the mathematicians to instruct us in the necessary elements of an equation that plots a curve not yet apparent?

We pretend to have given the magnolia tree a radiant energy and an expansive connection to young stars surrounded by gas and dust clouds.

*

We find ourselves turning again to consideration of a procedural reality, one that almost forces us to deny a possible physical reality.

*

We seem not to have learned a Wilsonian lesson concerning boundaries and compositional analogies, the complexities of reconstituted shape.

*

The apprentice now disdains our conflation of shape and form, holding the candle of the woman's body against the luminous form of the magnolia tree.

Nothing permits us to address the incoherence of absolute simplicity. Nothing permits us to argue the coherence embodied in our magnolia tree.

*

Bösendorfer wants to acknowledge a paradigmatic function to which our magnolia would submit. But could we dress our landscape in "matters of kinds," that is, a proposed construction that needs no geometrical binding?

*

How do we read Schrödinger's argument for entanglement, the interaction of two systems where the state function of the composite system no longer "factors into the product of the component state functions"?

The apprentice now shivers with disgust when she hears any parade of numbers. Perhaps her sympathies lie with Schrödinger and his worry over the incompatible measurement procedures for one of the two entangled systems, leading to what, to her, might be a false resolution of the entanglement.

*

Our beginning impressed a simplicity upon us, and we find ourselves struggling to impose a complicated order on procedures that threaten to have nothing to do with each other, no programme of observations that would offer formal resolution or relief.

*

Shall we give in to our apprentice?

Consider the flying hawk, a propositional eccentricity in our landscape. Therefore, we must deny our philosopher her move from apprenticeship to advocacy, even though our move skirts its own logic.

*

The ritualist understands the flexibility of rule.

*

Perhaps we might say that only the ritualist needs a sacred calculus.

*

Thinking on this, we should not involve Wilson in any tropospheric complacency, or a Leibnizian monadology, though we must scurry about to find a point of entry to a flexible façade.

*

We cannot escape Rotman's challenge to the real-number continuum and what he sees as the preeminence of linearity, continuity and infinity as scientific tools.

*

We must find a way of addressing a principle of decomposition that would engender another set of motivation in the ritualist, and that would occasion some form of reconciliation between Wilson's quiltwork assemblies and the individually studied and reassembled bits Rotman proposes.

*

The ritualist might now propose an efficient "linguistic engineering," a fracturing of descriptive tasks that would lead us to Holden's Kant, where a compositional doctrine threatens to spill over into an unsettling tropospheric complacency.

*

Our apprentice will not allow any mathematical aura to the ritualist. This denial argues a misunderstanding, an attempt to remove the ritualist from the geometrical complexities that the ritualist, in fact, inhabits.

*

We must remember Wilson's challenge to semantic finality. He would remind us that "concept" does not "behave in a rule-governed way across all its applications." The apprentice thinks she has caught *us* attributing a flexibility to "rule" that rule itself has not earned and cannot display.

*

Think on this: "... much of language's potential usage is likely to be currently *formless*, in that it is not yet settled how its terminology should be employed over domains as yet rarely visited."

*

We earlier had almost repudiated the mathematician's ability to instruct us in the necessary elements of an equation that would help us in restructuring a formless domain.

*

Bösendorfer would now repudiate the poet's metaphorical ambition.

*

We come close to overstepping boundaries that seem thoroughly reluctant to appear.

Can we come to terms with our poet's misprision of a perfectly functional intuition embodied in the notion of "property dragging"?

*

Consider this: The poet's imagination might give us the circular structure of nerve damage in the magnolia tree. Should we honor such imagination, treat it the way we would treat Wilsonian façades?

*

Certainly, our poet could argue for his conceptual misunderstanding, insisting that this simply marks new territory for a conceptual misunderstanding.

*

Can we argue, at the side of our poet, for a corrupt analysis that would make sense in an integral domain?

Where would we start the transformation of conceptual terms that have not overcome their formlessness? How could we focus upon a particular linguistic object that we cannot isolate?

*

Perhaps we could do better with number. But that suggests a linearity to number. That notion, surfacing here, would return us to Rotman, who contests the preeminence of linearity in our mathematics and challenges the idea of the sequence of natural numbers.

*

Our young philosopher has not figured a way to build upon that abstraction, has not come upon the programme that would satisfy the third term in the Bamoun esthetic, the "thématique," as proposed by Mveng.

Difference and incompatibility, notions that keep troubling the waters.

*

Shall we entertain Piet Mondrian's little book, *Réalité naturelle et réalité abstraite*? Would Wilson welcome it?

*

Who shall set whom against Prigogine's non-equilibrium source of order? Certainly, some will find solace in Austin's perlocutionary act, or bliss again in that synthetic incompatibility we found in Lord Russell.

*

We turn back to that Netherlandish conversation in a Paris studio.

*

What shall we make of this: "Dans l'art nous pouvons définir cette différence comme suit: l'art ancien est une représentation inconsciente d'harmonie par la conscience des choses matérielles, l'art nouveau au contraire est la représentation de rapports équilibrés par la conscience de l'esprit."

*

Our Augustinian woman at the magnolia disputes this sullen orthodoxy. She refuses to examine this singular magnolia as a variable quantity. She can only argue against a "certain understanding of pure iteration."

*

Perhaps our Augustinian woman has trafficked with those who oppose the light, and has become enamored of disorder, suspicious of a constant point of origin and a vibration that pretends to organize the world.

*

274 SOUL AND SUBSTANCE

Should we now look to that medieval mathematical practice signaled by Netz, one that aspires to order and completion?

*

But we cannot overlook that, among the Bamana, the guardian of souls remains capable of transformation, and the matter represented by tere reminds us of our contingency.

*

We must review our texts to trace this matter of contingency or its repudiation.

Can we pass, with the boli, these fabricated objects we have found near or within our magnolia, "from and through a theory of knowledge to fit a theory of being"?

*

What, for example, would clarify those fundamental notions that the sciences (physics, biology, psychology et al.), according to Levinas (after Husserl), do not?

*

Quine has, of course, repudiated any such "First Philosophy," arguing, indeed, for the thorough adequacy of Science to adjudicate its laws.

*

Wilson complicates our scene by citing, in his flight from inten-
sion, "There is no entity without identity, and the identity of
properties is ill defined."

*

Our apprentice wants to be naughty. She draws our attention to this: "But while the world of the physicist claims to go beyond naïve experience, his world really exists only in relation to naïve experience."

*

Would Wilson agree? Can Wilson admit the phenomenologist to our symposium?

*

Bösendorfer thinks our empiricists become antsy about sets or, perhaps more to the point, encounter some difficulty in tracing a line from a conception of properties to that other name (according to Quine), classes.

*

Why does this matter?

*

La matière et le vide s'entremêlent.

*

The child in the hollow has no conception of the absent fruit
the woman ascribes to the magnolia.

*

Strophe → antistrophe → epode

*

Can Parmenides' predicational monism ever satisfy, or challenge, Cantor's theory of aggregates, or sustain Rotman's argument against the mathematical infinite?

*

Dieterlen reports that Faro exists as a voice before becoming a body.

*

Shall we listen to Heaviside: "There is no self-contained theory possible, even of geometry considered merely as a logical science, apart from practical meaning. For a language is used in its enunciation, which implies developed ideas and processes already in existence, besides the general experience associated therewith. We define a thing in a phrase, using words. These words have to be explained in other words, and so on, forever, in a complicated maze. There is no bottom to anything. We are all antipodeans and upside down."

*

Bösendorfer catches himself punning on Quine's antipodean mark upon the phenomenologists' First Philosophy.

*

Our apprentice hears the ancient voice in the magnolia, and feels disturbed by a decomposition that has escaped her view. She now wants to quarrel with Laplace, who has set her a course of sets and partial differentials blinding her to this pantheon of particles.

*

Shall we call Hallett unjust when he tells us Cantor could never explain what constitutes unity or what constitutes a set?

*

What now could Parmenides' predicational monism have to do with the canonical aggregate, as defined by Cantor, as defined by Hallett?

*

"It is one of the fundamental principles of physics (indeed of all science) that experiments that are sufficiently separated in space have unrelated results. The probabilities for various collisions measured at Fermilab should not depend on what sort of experiments are being done at CERN at the same time. If this principle were not valid, then we could never make any predictions about any experiment without knowing everything about the universe."

*

At Pittsburgh they know, "predictive purpose is not the *sine qua non* of scientific intent; for most purposes, we prefer addressing chief practical questions by *avoiding* predictive tracking as best we are able"—a bit of linguistic wayfaring to consider.

*

Bösendorfer wants to remind us of the *simplest* and *most economical* abstract expression of facts with regard to the magnolia tree in twilight sun, a woman lit by paradox, an egg, a child's bundled body.

*

Wilson would here propose the "significance of 'follows rules that we understand through effective manipulation,'" perhaps sensing something operative propelled by "interfacial factors that lie outside our active awareness."

*

Sklar insists that "The general theory of relativity requires that many realistic physical situations result in the formation of singularities, giving rise to physical situations that, on the theory's own account, amount to a breakdown in the theory's ability to fully characterize its own domain of application."

*

Our apprentice deplores our indifference to her situation with regard to number. She finds the impurity of number aggressively designed by a checkerboard pattern that seems to have grown from an unfounded and unbounded division of space.

*

How will she read Iamblichus reading the Soul as it reads Logoi "as noetic completeness and as immediacy"? How will she confront such a text as this, "Now is a 'limit' that changes with the other and other of motion yet rests in single form"?

*

The Dogon tell us that *one* is disorder, destruction, incompleteness.

*

Wō: to be somewhere, to be or exist in a place. Rotman measures the significance of that, and turns toward an understanding of the magnolia tree's subversion, of the woman's subversion.

*

Rotman would start us on a "scheme of counting" and "constructing—significantly creating the numbers and interpreting them arithmetically," leading to a subversion, which might seem to shadow what the apprentice calls a prior subversion.

*

Nothing should allow a small conceptual turn, dressing the magnolia as boli. We would have to deny an absolute movement of diverse materials, the facticity of time.

*

The energetic interaction of scattered particles.

*

Here we must begin the compounding of event.

*

ēhyeē: the edge or limit of a plot of land—
        We think boundary;
        we think a differential
        fabrication of space;
        we think impurity
        in the measure of light.

*

Time, say the Akan, has no need for event.

Would Wilson find sufficient clarity and balance in the Dogon conception of the number two? Would he turn his tuned ear to Juan Carlos Bösendorfer's rehearsal at his balanced keyboard?

*

Our young philosopher will now argue that number, under any musical necessity, needs no argument to establish its breath.

*

Does our apprentice have an ear for music, or a body capable of opposing light?

Mveng wants us to remember the attentive adjustment of a body that did not arise with light.

*

Why should we believe in a poet who has no need for a generating symbol?

*

Why should we honor the ritualist who has discovered a constant point of origin and wants to keep it a secret?

*

What tells us Faro's secret, the world reconfigured as a spiral, and that vibration which must become the realized universe?

*

Have we abandoned Lord Russell?

Do we look for a continuity, or take that as the guilty notion that Rotman would advise us to avoid?

*

Will we ever get around the logician's proposal that every well-defined series of terms must have a last term? We would seem to have to face again the problem of order.

*

Our apprentice finds herself at odds with any presupposition of an absolute regularity in nature, and disputes the reality of a logical theory of number and a logical theory of continuity.

*

Have we abandoned Lord Russell?

The poet tries again to establish a generative relation that would make sense of time as an objective metaphysical existence beyond change, process, and event.

*

Bösendorfer resents the poet's entrance upon the ground that he, Bösendorfer, has established as his own. He senses a confounding signatum he swears the poet can never understand, or weave through any three-part or four-part division of space. For Bösendorfer, incompleteness reigns, and two remains an inaccessible number.

*

Our young philosopher might now ask for a definition of substance and of material bodies, willing to propose a Wilsonian enlargement of application.

*

Must Faro appear as the center of cardinal points? The poet recognizes the improvisatory and badly calculated (meaning poorly plotted) notion that can only lead to *that* Russell's synthetic incompatibility.

*

"We may say that a formula containing two variables and defining a function must, if it is to be practically useful, give a relation between the two variables by which, when one of them is given, all the corresponding values of the other can be found; and this seems to constitute the mathematical essence of all formulae."

*

Nothing here should speak of conjugation, the complexity of an Augustinian woman and an isolated magnolia tree.

*

Have we approached the problem of equilibrium? Should we take up again our first proposition with its relevant velocities, and accept light as a musical term?

*

Have we, through Nancy, composed our Augustinian woman as Nancy proposes we have composed our world?

*

Can we enlist Wilson to treat our magnolia tree apart from its temporal dimension? Could we enlist Lord Russell to establish a well-defined series consisting of the four propositional accounts we chose to notice, and then follow the trace that "remains withdrawn," without origin?

*

Bösendorfer wants to appeal to memory, and to the hymnal exigencies left unstated when our geometric ambition turned us from that first twilight movement.

*

When did our decomposition start, shadowed, contested, by a movement toward order and completion?

*

We find ourselves flummoxed by what we must recognize as a second-order expression emphasizing mathematical relations.

*

We feel undone by our ingenuity in turning a geometrical alignment into an ethical alignment, if not an argument.

*

No one in Pittsburgh will sustain this floating beyond the body, or approve of serving an intelligence that belongs to the body outside the body.

*

No one will forgive our letting an analytic temper lead us away from understanding.

*

Our apprentice protests the swiftness with which we seem to have dismissed the "localized opportunities" in taking entanglement as νόμος, pulling it, by property dragging, away from all closed universes.

*

What can we learn from this:
        *anoma no yē patu,
in the abstract domain we might want to establish?

    *(The bird is an owl. Akan)

We retreat into a membership that can only reveal itself by going beyond its limits.

*

"To exist does not mean the same thing in every region."

*

Can we assume that Quine has erased this sentence?

*

"L'être est un acte."

*

The woman at the magnolia might now insist upon an intuitive transcendent moment—call it act or event—without giving in to any tropospheric complacency.

*

The child in the tree's hollow thinks of the world as event, spiraling through "divergent modes of rhythmic behavior."

*

The child has learned his music from George Russell, and has accepted how sound "holds linear time captive."

*

We might almost say that our sheltered child solicits Rotman's appeal to the restructuring of number and Wilson's appeal to the manipulation of event, those elements that lead to constructive design of a dense and complex order which exists in the way that George Russell says it does—above time.

*

How can we convict that first configuration of slipping the knot of an applicable order without accepting its temporal relationships?

*

We find ourselves composed beyond our own limits, or limited by a composition without discernible origin, a function approaching numerical order with no material necessity.

*

And yet, we have this convocation around the woman, the child, and the magnolia, who seem to have traveled on their own recognizance through that special light to create a spiraling verticality that astonishes, and confounds our impropriety.

*

What can we say of the phenomenal nature of this silence?

The Tuning of Grammar and Syntax

The Village piper keeps trying to find the fit of ἀέσθησις and entanglement.

We must pretend to construct a topological distinction, or at least a fiction of experimental control.

Isabelle Stengers might like to prevent a Spinozistic demeanor.

Shall we begin our speech here with Weinberg's three con-
served quantities: electric charge, baryon number, lepton num-
ber, and the notion that all properties in a system of thermal
equilibrium find their values there?

Our apprentice wants to give herself to τό ἄπειρον and the
boundaries created by time.

The transcendental, companionable Bamana would like to
make space for Jane Harrison's three exhibition of sacra: what
we see, what we do, what we say.

How ingenious to place these altars in three: stumps, carved stone, boliw. The last of these suggest, according to the adepts, the complexity of value, situation, and time.

Consider that divine Bamana trio and their attributes, an organization of soul, conscience and contingency.

Our apprentice displays an affection for the contingency embodied in Mousso Koroni. Shall our scholar abandon Spinoza, who admits no contingency, and simply return to a universe conceived as a progression of thought?

Can we, with Faro, figure the world as a spiral (munu) where Faro occupies a constant point of origin, at the center of cardinal points?

Must we accept the spiral's vibration as a move to realize the materiality of the universe?

Roberto Jason Thalassinos enters to remind us of Philolaus and the notion that understanding something means understanding its structure and numerical ratio.

Thalassinos here probes our understanding that sensible objects "have number," and exhibit a rational structure determined mathematically, even though the sensible thing might change.

The piper recognizes an argument he might have overlooked as he read Knorr Cetina, as she addressed the constantly changing historical occurrences with which physicists deal through technology.

We must understand, as Knorr Cetina suggests, that that technology creates and exploits representations on three levels.

Thalassinos focuses upon the physicists' representational vocabulary, as given by Knorr Cetina—the reconstruction of events appearing as signs.

Have we come upon a first quarrel in our surgery that will have no resolution, one that takes us into a dangerous area of interpretation?

Stengers, addressing Carnot's fiction, proposes an active rationalization: "the physicist no longer seeks to construct a purified description of the phenomenon she studies, she constructs from whole cloth a fiction susceptible to objective description, able to describe how it should be described."

Stengers tells us that Carnot's object refers to work we can re-
quire of any physical-chemical process "providing we suppress
its 'natural' activity."

The phrase provokes the advocate to ask: shall we read 'natural'
as a priori? and how does the abstract agent, the suppressor,
choose its target?

Stengers will insist that the physicist does not address a set of
interacting objects evolving in spacetime but a fictional being
with an indifferently assigned temporal change.

Could we fit another argument, regarding the well-constructed fiction? We might hear this note, "for the perceptive experiences monads define, each for and by itself, are in harmony, as if they were different perceptions of the same world."

Sklar, questioning true representations of the world, offers the notion that a "fundamental physical theory is applicable to systems in the real world only after numerous crucial idealizations have been made."

Danger or disguise? The advocate drains the juice from that word, representation.

Mark Wilson offers his *essential idealization,* telling us that the physicist must *artificially intervene* with some basic conceptual structure of her own to impose upon "amorphous reality."

Should we welcome the disturbance of an intervention of such nature? Should we speak at all of an essential idealization?

Karen Barad offers support to our advocate, citing Bohr in his discussion of discontinuity and indeterminacy: "concepts are defined by the circumstances required for their measurement," Bohr's challenge (according to Barad) to the measurement transparency in Newtonian physics.

You will note that a small unit of grammarians struggles here with an unspoken (call it an uncovered) empiricism.

The apprentice continues to see offense in this statement: "the scientist must select some artificially crisp set of conceptual units to prime the pump of physical description upon whose basis she can then frame empirical descriptions of laboratory events."

We realize that we have set out in search not of a conceptual structure but of a function of order.

The piper recognizes a geometrical deficiency as well as a propositional debility. Nothing will repair an order that never appears.

Those in Santa Cruz would tell us *"theoretical concepts* are not ideational in character; they are specific physical entanglements."

Barad proposes, and our apprentice wants to accept that "measurement and description (the physical and the conceptual) entail each other."

Do not expect to find consolation in Weyl's assessment that "all a priori statements in physics have their origins in symmetry."

The piper would like to refuse his own deception, run away from Mark Wilson's amorphous reality.

He turns again to his *Symmetry*: "Relative to a complete system of reference not only the points in space but also all physical quantities can be fixed by numbers. Two systems of reference are equally admissible if in both of them all universal geometric and physical laws of nature have the same algebraic expression."

How now approach a topology that would teach an undiscovered space, an embellishment of fictions, or the fiction of embellishment, the di that activates and challenges form?

Do we argue with form or with our apprentice who must always have a language of form?

Nadler directs us to Proposition 16 of the *Ethics*, and proposes Spinoza's language shift. Shall we read that proposition with Elwes, as our apprentice seems determined to do, that last dramatic phrase, "things fall within the *sphere* of the intellect."

Has our problem at this point become a mathematical one or a clever analogy handled only by language?

Evelyn Fox Keller warns us against misusing what we might call "as if constructions," or rushing toward an absolute degree of resemblance between the world and our ambiguous logic.

Think of this as an evasion. "Critique du rythme, et pas critique de la théorie du rythme, c'est une fondation du rythme dans le langage, c'est-à-dire dans le sens, non à côté du sens."

Think on this: "A language . . . is not so much a set of sentences, or of sentence patterns, as a set of much smaller patterns of formation which in combination enable a speaker to produce sentence patterns."

Our linguists love the degrees of grammaticalness.

The piper feels a need to retain a conception of body and force, with two distinctions surrounding an active force, called primitive (inherent in every corporeal substance) or derivative (resulting from the limitation of the primitive force through the collision of bodies)—a lesson he learned through the particle hunters in spite of Moulago.

Along this way, we must encounter Leibniz following Galileo's "propensity to movement" of a heavy body in search of a dead force.

Should we now speak of displacement, the constant change in culture that affects our experimental practice?

Set at this point a boundless syntax and a quarrel with the soul.

The Bamana conceptual spiral must, in logical order, fall toward number, mako nyelanw, the things that arrange needs.

We might find it hard to resist Leibniz's non-extended metaphysical atom.

That point might surface in the geometrical exigencies of Proposition 29, and the devastation of a contingency Leibniz perhaps might defend.

The advocate begins the delineation of systems that will remain thoroughly inarticulate—an active dissonance the piper cannot bridge.

Nketia tells us that African traditions treat songs as speech, and suggests that musical phrases tend to correspond to grammatical structural units. That might argue for a coherence through prosody.

How shall we account then for musical patterns and terms that extend beyond regional boundaries?

We go too far, perhaps, in reading Leibniz (through Garber), "Extension or space and the surfaces, lines, and points one can conceive in it are only relations of order or order of existence . . ."

We have a choice: πλάζω to be led astray, or to accept "what is the case."

Mudimbe might urge us into a centrifugal ecstasy, a standing out of oneself, to be where one is not.

Here we should encounter a separation, a thorough disjunction.

Shall we return to Parmenides to investigate the small opaque white beads of Ọbàtálá (Òrìṣà-ńlá)?

Why believe in absolute power, or a potential present in all things?

Our combative philosopher wants to enlist Stengers against any Spinozistic closed system.

She has found, too, the beauty of that Arabic word qaṣīd, decomposed as q-s-d (qaṣd), calling up intention, purpose.

The village piper got himself involved with the beauty of nyi, obscurity, and would have liked to have called and to have wedded that perfect unchanging order in ma'at.

At times, the piper feels compelled to a Bastide rule, finding coherent expression in an operative equation—
religion = correspondence,
magic = accumulation.

The apprentice prefers to emphasize another Bastide notion—a mosaic syncretism inherent in social practice that gives not a simple fusion but the existence of disparate objectives.

Shall we argue now for batá in Ségou, or the paradoxical notion that Eboussi-Boulaga might misconstrue in Parmenides?

What gets lost if our measuring forces do not submit themselves to a single instrumentality? Have we buried a relevant measurement that exhibits a rational harmony?

Haven't we occasionally approached that enigmatic gem without a sufficient understanding, or the involvement, of time?

Time, according to the Akan, does not involve us, or need us—a notion that would lead to a perfect quarrel with Manchester.

Time sits upon us, or time sits within us, a shimmering semblance of undiscovered life.

"Time does not exist. All that exist are things that change. What we call time is—in classical physics at least—simply a complex of rules that govern change."

The clever advocate goes searching Aristoxenus:
>ταξις χρόνων ἀφωριξμένη
>Rhythm is an ordering (or a defined ordering) of time.

What do we make of this, if we consider Hugo Riemann's address (through Christopher Hasty) to Aristoxenus:

"Time is not, after all, itself divided, rather for the articulation of the lapsing of time is required a materially perceptible Other to carry out this articulation . . ."

Musical Aristoxenus wants to treat with memory.

How now address that path through which one kind of particle converts into another?

Call this a wandering significance. We seem to have stumbled into a complexity we had thought to avoid: the duplicity inherent in the performance of a ritual text.

Time confounds us still, brings a problem of the homogeneity of nature, its "language," its conceptualization.

We must recall that Mudimbe insists that Dogon myth remains a "powerful organization of classifications, filiations and transformations," and urges sight beyond formal systems to unveil other symbolic networks.

Our apprentice wants to appear naughty. She reminds us that kórè rituals among the Bamana deride figures of learning and power.

How reconcile this with the belief that all phenomena present themselves as "signs to be interpreted," and how begin an exploration of dyako, an embellishment that gives form an identity in spacetime?

We seem to have turned upon ourselves, looking for time's precision, the continuity assumed in its making, the contestable assertion that events follow upon or fail.

"One can think of space and time as being composed of events; the collection of all events encompasses all of space and time."

The piper has to restrain his admiration for such an elaborate measure of gravity.

Shall we listen to Manchester? "Origin within the Boundless is gravity, downward motion, converging toward center. . . . Syntax is the form of the inward agreement of gravity and time. Its most perfect utterance is silence."

We skirt away from this inelastic scattering—a motion that appears to sustain a tropospheric complacency we ought at least to deny.

You have to see that, along the way, we let contingency prevail, circumventing those "complex rules that govern change."

The apprentice now proposes Russell's solution to a predication problem, trying to defend the order of generating new propositions.

Have we now unwittingly returned to that non-extended meta-physical atom? Have we gone beyond any conception of body and force?

Shall we deny any express universal movement, any constituting force, any confabulation of "duration and space"?

Eboussi-Boulaga resists our attempt to reinstate force as a natural function, a notion that circles and perhaps establishes a dynamism Eboussi-Boulaga finds it difficult to accept.

The piper thinks he has uncovered a misspelling in Proposition 16 and the corollary to Proposition 32, a double logos leading mischievously toward an ontology.

Our Spinozistic Jean-Loup Amselle insists that myth-ritual practices among the Bamana (and one might add the Dogon, Senufo, Mossi) do not constitute systems.

The piper owns himself inattentive to a resonance he overlooked while considering Dieterlen's unfolding of a Bamana sensible universe conceived as progression of thought.

The difficulty might have arisen when the analyst ignored the concept tere, or more probably split it from any notion of conscience.

We pause at the entrance to this path—that second, or third, look at the rebellious Mousso Koroni with her opposition to light, and creative disorder.

Our grammarians go searching for sustenance, reading Peter Pesic in his approach to Michael Faraday and attending to the expression that makes matter "nothing but forces and the lines in which they are exerted."

We should at this point rehearse our Greek, ἡ ἐνέργεια, an action, operation, energy.

Our physicist urges us to think of ἐνέργεια as en-acted, the doing of a thing.

If we go further into Faraday (through Pesic) we mark a passage for which we should find an interpretation: "light radiation is a higher species of vibration in the lines of force which are known to connect particles and also masses of matter together."

May we call upon Faro and his struggle with materiality?

Stengers orders us down another path. The advocate, mathematical and responsively physical, wants to examine the impact of Stengers's = sign, addressing the identity of a system throughout its "representational changes."

Where have we arrived, if not at the possibility of a dynamic system Eboussi-Boulaga must set against a Parmenidean equilibrium?

Nothing says that any of these systematic ratios will submit to temporal change; nor will anyone committed to a system of energetic articulation know how to accommodate points "stripped of any mutual interaction."

Questions proliferate around any possible configuration that might recall us to that constantly surfacing monad.

We seem to have skipped away from nyama or masiri, a purpose activated by a causal equality.

How would Mousso Koroni approach a distinction between absolute and radiant luminosity, given the mosaic syncretism of the teleo-theological activity she displays in her legislative role?

Will our advocate now try to move us toward the idea of an abstract agent?

The piper wants to defer this talk of any agency, preferring to turn our attention to Spinoza's closed system (as Stengers would have it), his elimination of a barrier between the observer (subject) and observed (object), a notion conceptually similar (according to Mendel Sachs) to Galileo's Sun-centered universe.

Haven't we traveled with Galison through the inner labora-
tory, and learned there that the passage of time changes too
much about the nature of the laboratory and experimenta-
tion for a "typical" experiment to capture the "principles" of
experimentation?

Note, too, how, in spite of our intransigently inclined advocates'
assaults on that topos, the inner laboratory (comprehensively
defined) remains a touchstone of inquiry, if for no other reason
that it reminds us of constraint.

Ut pictura poesis. Could we say the same about theory?

Our apprentice, half in love with theory, disdains any quarrel with the notion of its materiality.

Think on it. One might get stripped in Ségou following Dalilu, standing near the cornerstones of state religion and power.

What does that have to do with a mosaic syncretism and signification?

Speak of danger, we come close to it here. We struggle to get above religions, social and political categories, though the image of a pot of purifying water and these altars built of red/ white stones and a stripped segment of the root of a mahogany tree (jala; *Khaya senegalensis*) remains.

We might overlook the blacksmith/sculptor, discount a source of special energy, an intrinsic, technical power.

We have to deal with that first transformation: Mousso Koroni become Nyalé, the mother of all transformations, the first to possess a soul.

The apprentice will emphasize Nyalé's energy, impetus, desire, secrecy and disorder, and claim all in contrast to the Andoumboulou, charging this perhaps to her double, Faro.

We will find ourselves encouraged to consider that doubling as an essential attribute, one of equilibrium.

The art of the newborn, a relevant measurement that demands a rational harmony.

What outrage could follow? What has our = sign done?

"Cause and effect are reciprocally self-determining. Cause is not responsible for effect . . . its identity is derived solely from the relationship of conservation it shares with that effect."

Must we, can we, do away with causal equality in assuming that cause enters another set, disappears?

Thalassinos does not know how to treat such logic; the piper feels he has lost his grasp of the very grammar and syntax he set out to approve.

We seem to have traveled through this forest, following Stengers following Leibniz following Galileo's "propensity to movement" of a heavy body. What did we overlook? The definition of a dead force, a force that would occur if the body lost all restraint.

The point seems to lie elsewhere.

Consider Murdoch's description of Bohr's "correspondence principle," which Murdoch takes as a generalization of implications of Bohr's theory of the hydrogen atom, a principle that Bohr intended (according to Murdoch) "to operate as a methodological rule to guide formulation of laws in quantum theory."

The piper finds himself at a loss to place the principle.

Can we return to that motion "that is continuously being born and continuously canceled," and look for a transition to the "singularity of the dynamic state"?

At this point, Mujynya's four principles of ontological dynamism enter to confound any authentic Scotian reference that presents a separate measure to "test a simple concept for its truth or falsity."

Do we here deal with different states of a dynamic object?

Oh, such wandering significance. Think of Eboussi-Boulaga and Engelbert Mveng sketching a Greek geometrical practice into a mendable mathematics of being.

We seem to have stepped outside our productive domain, and to have forgotten the utility of the multidimensional concept of fiction we have found in Galison, Sklar, Wilson, Knorr Cetina, along with the improbability of theoretical and experimental purity.

What would Popper's conception of particle matter propensity have to do with the existence of these simultaneous levels of explanation?

The apprentice tries to obviate our walking away too soon from an investigation of experimental control and a sure conception of phenomena.

You can see a wounded attempt to establish a ritual context as a methodological control, to interpret the transfer of energy and momentum between "one quantity of matter (the 'measured') and another quantity of matter (the 'measurer')."

We have borrowed that notion from Sachs to focus upon new terms—observational, relational, interpretive—as they enter and turn our attention to procedures that have been set aside when addressing the experiment of ritual, causing us to overlook the functional order of its inquiry.

Galison's notion of the inner laboratory suggests we might find a duplicate form of an inner laboratory.

Thalassinos argues for a principle. He begins a provocative
reading: "no well-defined use of the concept 'state' can be
made ... referring to the object separate from the body with
which it has been in contact, until the external conditions in-
volved in the definition of this concept are unambiguously fixed
by a further suitable control of the auxiliary body."

Have we come upon a misreading or the beginning of a parallel
reading applicable only to our notion of ritual experimentation?

The analyst must find that box experiment that here will give the
same state of physical reality and not an account of two different
phenomena.

What would go missing? The judgment that we can only concern ourselves with "a discrimination between different experimental procedures which allow of the unambiguous use of complementary classical concepts."

Where has the piper landed with his repudiated force that refuses its annihilation as a creative, or shall we say created, phenomenon?

We must now confront that tangled notion in Burkert where he argues that "number is not quantity and measurability, but order and correspondence, the articulation of life in a rhythmical pattern, and the perspicuous depiction of the whole as the sum of its parts."

The piper shudders remembering a faint resolution in rhythm's definition.

Thalassinos would like to rescue this assertion, bring it into that "geometrical algebra" of Greek/Babylonian calculation.

Burkert resists, and offers a further complication: "Number in fact means restraint; counting is performed in successive acts, and thus time itself, composed of successive events, is number."

Our defensive campaign against time seems to have put us in a trick. What can we salvage here?

Read this carefully: "The great mass of the Akusmata had to do with sacrificial ritual, and its methods and times, the καιροί, so that correct piety (εὐσέβεια) depends on knowing number."

Have we lost anything here?

Consider this from Pesic: "Arithmetic relies on the most fundamental insight into being and otherness and how they can be combined into more or less inclusive wholes when considered as a one, or distinguished into the various numbers as many."

Pesic emphasizes the primal category of multitude in whole numbers, each one called an arithmos, and draws us into seeing counting as essential to the performance of sacred ritual.

We remind ourselves of a Wittgensteinian puzzle: une sophie, un ensemble, ordonné $\longrightarrow$ 22 categories, 12 elements (264) each one head of a list of 22 pair, 11,616 signs $\longrightarrow$ the mathematical insinuation of a variable system sò: váduru, the extended word, the final detail of abstraction.

Think now of rhythm, as Pesic here does, as a shape or pattern conveying motion.

Think, too, of the common translation of motion into number among the Bamana, Dogon, Mossi, Senufo, Yoruba, Akan, and other μαθηματικοί energetically embraced by our astringent apprentice.

We must remember that every body presents a challenge to symmetry and equilibrium.

One might argue that a mode of knowledge might exist only as rupture or as a point of origin for further disruption and discontinuity.

Here, for example, what can we make of Rotman's suggestion that numbers "are things in potentia . . . theoretical availabilities of sign production"?

Πλοκή, lovely word that gives the sense of twining, weaving, the salutary dimension of complexity.

Could we take it as a cosmological skill exhibited by the μαθηματικοί of the Dogon, Yoruba, Bamana, Akan, and others?

ἀγωγή, lovely word that reminds of a passage from one consonance directly to another. Think of it as a carrying away, as a bringing to, or in.

Mathiesen's Cleonides turns us to a consideration of four compositional elements: ἀγωγή (sequence), πλόκη (succession), πεττεία (repetition), τονή (prolongation). Nothing there seems certain, even though the note might bring a functional order.

But, here now, what if we changed our inquiry to look at a constellation of symbols common to myth and art, the pairing, multiplicity, checkerboard pattern emphasized among the Dogon, as Barbara DeMott instructs us.

The apprentice urges caution with the derivation of a complex cosmogony that gives a vertical, three-part division of space, and a horizontal, four-part division of space.

How can we approach the Rotman number as a theoretical presence, a sign production?

The apprentice questions our syntax, and reminds us that Rotman argues for mathematics as process.

She would return us to the three semiotic routes defined by Rotman: referential (through the external world), formal (through material signifiers), psychological (through prior meanings).

The sympathetic piper insists that our apprentice misses Rotman's more substantive point—that "numbers no longer simply *are*, either in actuality or in some idealized potentiality: they are materio-symbolic or technosemiotic entities that have to be *made* by materio-symbolic creatures."

The apprentice turns the argument toward her annoyance with Rotman for his repudiation of Leibniz; as such she considers Rotman's treatment of alphabetic seriality.

She has refused Rotman's nomad number as serial continuation (rhythm, ordinality, melody) which he sets against parallel presentation (cardinality, harmony).

The piper wants to avoid these spiritually embracing definitions. He wonders what Rotman would do with Russell's statement that the generation of new propositions *must lie outside* the totality.

How would Rotman address Pesic's Pythagoreanism that posits an autonomy in each degree of freedom in a system because of the totality of the system?

Read this carefully. "This, then, is the perfect physical-mathematical realisation of the world of Leibnizian monads, which can be said to be causa sui and a faithful local expression of the universe they compose together."

Have we walked into Peirce?

"Anything, whatever, be it quality, existent individual, or law, is an icon of anything, in so far as it is like that thing and used as a sign of it."

Would Peirce approve of Rotman's treatment of symbol? Would he approve of Rotman's treatment of sign?

Let us step back for a moment: Has Rotman read Leibniz's statement that a "monad is windowless" in the way that our apprentice has read it?

The piper stands astonished by the perplexity of an inferred grammar/syntax.

He thought he could escape such perturbation by attending only to those elements manifested in syntactical form, made present by implied rules in composition, or the explicit inversion of a standard form.

Can he now explore all forms of difficult realization, which a pertinent syntax might transform into softly realized forms?

What does the piper understand? Consider this: "In no instance can there be any justification for 'understood' elements or deletion transformations except in the STRUCTURE of the language."

Our small unit of grammarians appears too willing to leap boundaries, too willing to provide rules for structural patterns that we can treat as languages.

We seem to have forgotten all and salutary configurations of singularities, all our skepticism about all that we, in our dynamic existence, must find operationally undiscoverable.

The apprentice accuses the piper and his constituents of intractable and unsavory dimensions that only compromise the notion of a hierarchy of structural patterns.

She has excavated this notion, and, referring as example to language, she insists upon a hierarchy of systems.

The piper knows he has met these notions before, and refuses this legacy of grammars.

The representational realists do not like the way we throw away our principles; they deplore the manner in which we have avoided a useful definition of phenomena.

These realists find our inability to understand a stated convergence that derives from Whiteheadian process theory, where we learn to treat potentiality as ontologically significant, reprehensible.

The awkwardness of our explanation belies the Bohrian simplicity by which we thought to move into an understanding of the multiplicities of logical space.

Will the sign pull us there? We had almost forgotten the mathematical materiality we thought beyond dispute.

"A sign must have signification, but it need not *denote* anything."

The advocate resents what she calls our algebraic audacity, and the way, in our sacramental contexts, we tie our measuring apparatuses to the observed event.

You must see exaggeration in this failing as the advocate proposes it, "What is perceived aesthetically may, but need not be a sign."

The piper recalls his intent to fit ἀέσθησις and entanglement. Would any description of a classically conceived observable help?

We feel abandoned by Spinoza, the Spinoza who tells us that our knowledge "is merely probable, but not certain."

The advocate has caught us skirting the necessity of finding any value in conserved quantities, refusing any topological distinction.

The piper could find his instrumental review in disarray. Lovely words surface, and then go into hiding, change their compositional significance.

Why dance again in this nafolo environment, if only to recall the "extensive continuum" that "expresses the solidarity of all possible standpoints throughout the whole process of the world."

Whitehead insists that "It is not a fact prior to the world; it is the first determination of order—that is, of real potentiality arising out of the general character of the world."

Should we look, at this point, for fundamental forms; an alphabet; a testing measure; internal, systematic harmonies?

Thalassinos arrives to provoke us into uncertainty, into that multiplicity of possible meanings for each sign our ritual experiment provides.

Thalassinos asks, what does it feel like to find yourself on a page like this, a curvature in space, accountable, but another figure unimaginable as substance?

Page and air conjoin to remind Roberto Jason Thalassinos of his displacement. Does that mean he has displaced Being? Does that mean he has removed himself from Being, or has substituted himself for Being?

Gyekye disturbs Thalassinos, confounds the piper and angers the apprentice. He insists that we have no direct equivalent of the noun "existence" in Akan, a language that questions existence as an attribute.

Shall we read?

> wō   to be somewhere, to be in place
> hō   there
> wō hō = there is
> "the existential verb involves location."

Consider this. Brett-Smith tells us, "Creating a basi, or working on a natural substance to endow it with power, requires that the ritual specialist or sculptor undertake physical procedures that rearrange the forces believed to be continually at work in the world of the dead and of spirits."

Brett-Smith reminds us that nyama, though it stands as a source of moral reciprocity (an "energy of action"), cannot be recreated.

We must note the mythic connection (taking into account the danger and necessity of blacksmiths) among anvil, iron ore, and humans.

"Les signes connotent un mot, une expression, un nombre de phrase."

We seem to have abandoned our exploration of signs, to have got ourselves in a fix over laada, negotiations with the spirit world "for access to the generative potential encapsulated in the ritual object."

Consider now: the owner of a Kọmọ mask does not own it; the mask, through sacrifice and exacting prescriptions owns the owner, who functions only as its guardian.

Have we forgotten the instrumental utility of signs, their multiplication?

The piper has become distressed by the notion that signs derive their depth and power by being subject to destruction.

Have we gone too far? The piper, seeking a mathematical distribution of the sun's light, sees it as a question of displacement and movement.

What could Pickering do, facing the observable solstices and equinoxes of the sun measured by taking bearings using three mono (meeting) altars placed west of the Upper Ogol (corresponding to three solar positions)—a measurement taken four times a year by the head of the ginna, in order to measure the direction of time?

What ontological movement requires a syntax?

We must address Pickering's "experimenters' 'theoretical construct,'" the tuning by which they adjust their techniques "according to their success in displaying phenomena of interest."

But our Galison wants to establish that observation remains independent of all theory, and will not take theory as the inductive limit of a series of prior experimental observations.

Has the piper learned the value of a cluster decomposition?

That vertically placed stick on the mono altars does not subscribe to any structuralist theory.

We have been dancing through order, holding everything as related by structure, indifferent to the success of a theory in its predictions.

The piper does not know how to propose an experimental function subject to justification by the experimenting ritualists of his regard, or how to propose the critical notion of a system of relations or patterns as structure as an epistemological method.

Can we say that we have arrived, with Resnik, at the limits of logic, and therefore agree that logical truth, consistency and implication "are not metaphysical properties and relations"?

The piper loves to travel, loves the disorientation of finding himself doubled and circumscribed, moving and finally coming to rest.

All this movement seems retrograde—altars that grow out of hymns, palimpsestic cities, a language written on broken headstones.

You can see that this story could get grimmer and dimmer, especially if, unlike the piper, the apprentice and Roberto Jason Thalassinos, you pay no attention to proportion, that quality of ratios that proposes your soul.

The piper begins with this: he knows his body, as with all mathematical objects, incomplete.

An Examination of Rhythm
and Its Expansive Movement

We might begin with a sure distinction in Polya, taken from Euclid, that will tell us that all arguments proceed in the same direction: (a) from data toward the unknown, and (b) from hypothesis toward a conclusion.

The Village piper thinks this badly stated, or, let us say, the piper thinks the first assertion here lacks rhythm. He refuses to make rhythm a solvable problem, and refuses to talk about procedure in rhythm.

One might think that the piper has lost his footing here, or has entered on the wrong foot. You might have already caught him introducing a problem that only a linguistic turn might satisfy.

Here we have begun a diabolic contest with form, something we could have learned in contemplating Netz on the shaping of deduction in Greek mathematics. We seem ourselves to be on the point of almost an indefensible assertion about the shape of rhythm. What is it?

We have moved rather swiftly into a spatial action we have not begun to specify. Do we treat rhythm as we do gravity, living with its manifest effects but never understanding it?

There we have already contaminated our own method. Our apprentice turned dozent knows the first difficulty for our inquiry remains embodiment.

Talk of the wrong foot. What can we say when we can offer no consensus on rhythm? Could we get by through some experimental measure that would lead to an entangled construction, a completeness only realizable through our constructive abilities when counting?

Can we even talk that way?

The dozent wants to examine our speech again. She asks us to consider what we thought we could avoid by living in number, but she will not let us have this escape, and puts us face up to the fictional appearance of temporal values.

What does the dozent offer us? "*Theoretical concepts* are not ideational in character; they are specific physical entanglements . . . measurement and description (the physical and the conceptual) entail each other."

The Village piper wants to misread Netz with regard to Greek geometrical propositions. What can we now make of this: "each geometrical proposition sets its own universe, which is its diagram"?

We float in an atmosphere that might only appear ceremonial. Shall we start again by listening to Alain-Michel Boyer, speaking of *Les Arts d'Afrique,* "Que nul n'entre ici s'il n'est géomètre. Tant de sculpteurs africains pourraient prononcer cette célèbre formule grecque, à voir le primat qu'ils accordent à des figures régulières: rectangles, triangles, cercles."

Boyer emphasizes line, oval, losange, cone, trapezoid, quadrilateral in the making. He finds no pure circle, and insists that we will find all angles fluid and supple.

Why pay attention here?

Komolo tébou, the four-armed bird, the creator god turned toward sky and earth, and the circular movement of the dance, figures "le visage du masque."

Will we find the movement leading us to a fundamentally intransigent notion and a fundamental failure?

We will have to go scouting the dual nature of time proposed by the Akan. Have we leapt into the tangle of an undefinable event? Can we, at this point, think of progression—the conceptualization of a phenomenon that won't stand still?

We catch ourselves playing with stillness.

We hardly know where to begin in this dance. We have to avoid circumscribing our inquiry by keeping it close to certain fundamental notions of the body's engagement we pretend to understand.

The piper at times forgets his purpose. Thalassinos will always come to remind the piper that he, the piper, too easily abandons his own praxis.

We seem to have come to a workshop that will manifest a bee's hive of the body's burdens and boundaries, the bright disappearance of the mind.

The piper tries to find an excuse in treating his praxis as indefinable, lacking the substance to sustain, on its own, the linguistic turn we pretend to require.

What about these deeds and events that will not tell us about themselves? Can we live without a necessary reconciliation? You hear, of course, the dozent's meritorious howling.

Rhythm wants nothing, has nothing from Dante, no moto spirital.

We want to talk about this designable event that has us here enthralled. To do this, we have to repudiate an enthralling stillness, and perhaps unveil, as Mudimbe counsels us to do, other symbolic networks that would help to overcome the constraints of systems we have set in place.

The piper has his support. Think of Pesic reporting Riemann's remarkable statement given in the Dichten von Hypothesen— the poetry of hypothesis, urging us into an imaginative freedom, unrestricted by anatomic presuppositions.

Do not think of this as a Bamana kórè ritual set to deride figures (material and human) of learning and power. No, we look for that experimenter's theoretical construct, that tuning which will display phenomena of interest, something we have learned from Pickering.

Can we go as far as Danto: Every idea licenses an ontological argument? Or follow him in this: . . . sentences may suffer alteration in truth-value without sustaining alteration in, or loss of meaning?

The piper thinks of rhythms—the many variations of the proposition—and of time. He gets caught trying to understand Gyekye's relating of okra (soul) and sunsum (spirit), preparing himself to walk the dense forests of form and feeling, looking for that concrete reality that bere expresses.

"But the formulation we are considering concerns not the measurement of time but its nature 'in itself,' with respect to which it is called 'duration.' On this level, time is involved not in the motions of sensible things, but in their being, as it is subject to motion."

We must remember that Barbour wants us to remember that Leibniz contends that only things exist, and that the supposed framework of space and time represents a derived concept, a construction from things.

The piper tries to shelter in an absurd notion he pretends to derive from Jean-Luc Nancy that the world is not produced but "traced by that which remains withdrawn and by the withdrawal of an origin."

Thalassinos cautions the piper; proposes modesty and proportion when approaching that lumen.

Our dozent, who has already objected to the piper's fraudulent analogical method, regarding rhythm and gravity, joins Thalassinos in warning the piper against his own theology.

What use can the piper make of this: "There is a prima facie case for the proposition that arithmetic is no less a model for the structure of time as it governs actual or actualizable process than geometry is a model for empirically presented extension in space."

Our advocates like to argue with each other. We might have started with Pickering's "experimenters' theoretical construct," looking for a continuity that might never appear.

What does the piper want? How can he confront Attridge's "In their capacity to embody a range of mental conditions, rhythmic forms are . . . over-determined, and it is perhaps part of their function in poetry to broaden the scope of purely lexical meanings by relating them to a less specific substratum of affective energy"?

Have we stumbled upon an intrinsic architecture? The piper thought he had done away with the idea of rhythm as a solvable problem, and now finds himself involved in facing a "function of *world-disclosure*" and a general propositional knowledge of the world.

We must note Frege's need for the construction of a perfect formal language for sciences.

Think of the piper's astonishment when he finds that his colleague, the trustworthy dozent, now speaks of establishing a domain of perfect bodies within imperfect structures.

We have to take shelter in Mark Wilson's challenge to semantic finality, going along with the idea that "'concept' does not behave in a rule-governed way across all its applications."

We have already had the dozent's challenge to rule's flexibility. Where do we stand?

Following Wilson, we enlist the formlessness of language's potential usage, the unsettled employment in "domains rarely visited."

The problem here—that is, this prelude to a larger problem—comes about because the piper had earlier repudiated any mathematician's ability to instruct us in the necessary elements of an equation that would help us in structuring or restructuring a formless domain.

Should we think of rhythm as a formless domain, shaped by improvisatory shaping of space, sound, or any other relevant properties?

There you have it. My friend, Bösendorfer, turns up to repudiate my "poet's metaphorical ambition." He thinks I need a conceptual misunderstanding to lead me to a new territory for conceptual misunderstanding.

Let us turn to our dozent who does not allow a mathematical aura to the ritualist, an attempt to remove the ritualist from the geometrical complexities the ritualist inhabits.

Would our dozent listen to Kahn, who tells us, "The Milesian conception of the world as a geometrical organism suffused with life is thus the true archetype of the ancient point of view, the stimulus of all modern endeavors (such as those of Leibniz and, more recently, A. N. Whitehead) to interpret the total process of nature in terms of organic life"?

The piper keeps swinging around the idea that rhythm cannot be defined and yet needs defining in some way that would show us its organic life.

Where could we possibly begin to understand the phenomenon we call rhythm if we do not begin with the discernment of activity, motion, pressure, substance and other functioning attributes, all contributing to physical (then psychical) presence of intangible qualities strung on specifically tangible qualities?

How we wish for Graves and his explication of Gwion's heresy.

Did we say architecture? The piper seems to have an urge toward a structural sequence that would bring about that linguistic turn he thinks our inquiry needs.

Why should he turn so readily to Gyekye's exposition of that Akan active, spiritual and absolutely uniform world?

How far can we go to establish this unruly concept, rhythm, as a malleable form that establishes a new identity in this world, one that speaks to an identity in shape-shifting?

402 SOUL AND SUBSTANCE

We would then have to define an etic motive for rhythm. Something Merriam says we cannot do. Or perhaps we have intentionally misconstrued his argument.

But we were on our way to a functioning sequence that would help us make sense of a configuration that will not lie still for examination.

We must slip away from that soul that proposes Logoi as noetic completeness, and avoid all quarrel with immediacy.

But have we come to Eboussi-Boulaga's récit pour soi? Mudimbe might call this something put forward by "the rationality of historical sequences," and Eboussi-Boulaga will say "the récit is a reconstruction of history."

Looking more closely, we come upon a statement that threatens its own inertia: "By necessity a negation of the present, and also of the self, it is, at the same time, the only critical way to the self. Its internal dynamism will, eventually, guarantee the reconciliation of the historical reason and a reasonable freedom for Muntu."

Muntu, being of intelligence, corresponds (to those who declare such) to Aristotelian substance.

How could we now define that concept of form, schema, a purely perceptual, outward shape?

What will we do with Gyekye's insistence that time is an objective metaphysical existence, and real even if there are no changes, processes, events?

The Village piper wants to question the possibility of order in rhythm, marking the question of continuity. He once again wants to establish a generative relation that would make sense of time as "an objective metaphysical existence beyond change, process, and event."

But didn't our piper begin his inquiry by appealing to an abstraction? And didn't he appeal, by implication, to Rotman's restructuring of number and Wilson's manipulation of event?

The Dogon tell us that *one* is disorder, destruction, incompleteness. The piper wants to agree, wants, in spite of himself, to skirt the Akan, Manchester, Kubik, Mujynya, who will continue to argue the idea that no rhythm can be self-fulfilled, or satisfied with a relationship that leads to a single form.

Consider Rotman's "scheme of counting," his constructing and significantly creating the numbers and interpreting them arithmetically.

The piper calls this submission, shadowing what the dozent calls a prior subversion.

Time, say the Akan, has no need for event.

Can there be an empty casing for "an energetic interaction of scattered particles"?

We approach ēhyee: the edge or limit of a plot of land. We think of this with respect to rhythm: boundary, differential fabrication of space, impurity in the measure of light (sound). Euler already had us on edge.

Wilson alerts us to Yasumasa Nishiura, and the notion of the placements of boundaries that carry a great burden in descriptive work. Wilson quotes, "When we discern a wide variety of shapes, we are actually observing their boundary or perimeter. The boundary is exactly the place where the state (phase) of the matter changes abruptly, or, in other words, observing the boundary enables us to grasp the shape as a whole. Information is, so to speak, concentrated on the perimeter."

Can we awaken our piper to boundary, limit, or the bothersome problem of equilibrium?

We do not know whether to follow Russell in an understanding of a "well-defined series consisting of four propositional accounts."

Why follow that trace that remains withdrawn, without origin? Dangerous propositions arise; rhythm remains withdrawn from its own activity and cannot and/or will not specify its origin in any body.

Can rhythm choose its form of activity? Is there any improvisatory character being asked to balance, to fill gaps, to release a different movement from any already begun?

We seem to want to give in to what Netz recalls as a medieval urge. How use this, "When did our decomposition start, shadowed, contested, by a movement toward order and completion"?

If we want to scuttle time, as the piper seems prepared to do, that would make our inquiry into rhythm impossible.

You must notice Bösendorfer's dance on the piper's grave. He, Bösendorfer, reminds us that he has already demonstrated that incompleteness reigns, and two has become an inaccessible number.

Our dozent deplores our indifference to her situation with regard to number. She reminds us that she has found the impurity of number aggressively designed by a checkerboard pattern that seems to have grown from an unfounded and unbound division of space.

You would expect Bösendorfer now to pick at her soul and read it out of its ancient urgency.

But that would be an argument with Barbour, who claims that "time is linear, has an arrow, and is inferred from things."

Can Gyekye now accept such aid, as we feel has been offered here, laying time in the arms of an essentially phenomenal world?

What does that do for our dozent, and for the piper, looking for a rule to rule that will soon find itself abandoned?

The dozent moves from a significant notion of a governable—we might even say a measurable—event to the difficulty of specifying what (if anything) is in motion.

Can we even speak of a framework where we find these events embedded?

We want to extend the range of rhythm. You have to see the contradiction in extending the range of an entity that has given no evidence of extension.

Forgive us our debts. We have already tried to ride with a fraudulent analogical method, taking advantage of the silence of light, as Bösendorfer would have it.

Should we have said, the stillness of sound, and have set ourselves upon an exploration of the stressed syllable and a determination of meaning and syntax?

Somewhere along the way we must come to terms with the shape of sign structure, and the way that rhythm, however we conceive it, appears as a malleable form that establishes a new identity or speaks to an identity in shape-shifting.

How do we handle this? The Bamana tell us that Faro existed as a voice before he appeared as shape. Our dozent refuses to give in to such a conception. She calls this shapeless voice a trace too difficult to prepare or share.

Bösendorfer leaps in to remind us of our silly disposition of time, and questions once again the piper's Aristotelian praxis, which the piper might deny by turning away from any outward deed or event.

The dozent quietly asks us to face that lost linguistic turn that should account for any lost symmetry in the piper's account.

The piper pauses a moment to take into account his own distributions and model, his own use of variables. He cannot brave the modality hidden in Muntu, all notions related to modification of being in itself.

The dozent stops this motion. She has never come to terms with the flamboyant idea that *existing* cannot be used as a synonym for being there, cannot accept Mulago's sense of an ontological hierarchy in all existing beings.

Bösendorfer wants to rescue a certain discretion, a certain fundamental order before it escapes.

The dozent accuses us all of having forgotten the point of this story, that "visage du masque" which will always propel this inquiry.

The piper feels he must appeal to Mark Wilson for a "constructive design of a dense and complex order" that the piper perceives without accepting temporal relationships.

Thalassinos returns now in order to propose his own adherence to a distinction he might have misconceived. He wants to say with Meschonnic that we do not have a pluralité of rhythms but a pluralité of rhythm.

The dozent deplores this deviational scaffolding, calling it a sop to the piper, who keeps playing for an applicable order, even though he has lost the sense of this: "Le rythme est une mise en ordre déterminé des temps."

The piper does not know what to do with his need for understanding Stengers's fictional being, one with an indifferently assigned temporal charge.

A node arises here with this unspecifiable time, an unneeded time. How could the piper phrase what he has learned, or has persuaded himself, to see "the depth given to or drawn from an act embodied and subject to unspecified time."

> "Le Rythme est dans le temps ce que la symétrie est dans l'espace."

"Car le rythme est tout de même d'abord *périodicité perçue*."

The piper wants to argue, with Langer, against a common assumption (particularly in the sciences) "that the essential character of rhythm is the repetition of any distinct, recognizable event at equal intervals of time."

Perhaps we mean to contest the idea of elementary pulse units that never become strictly periodic.

It seems that the Village piper, at least, has misunderstood a presentational abstraction embodied in Faro, and has tried to tune his instrument to look for a series of successive levels of abstraction.

How has the piper dug himself that hole? Could he have avoided it by listening to Hans Hofmann, "Expansion and contraction in a simultaneous existence is a characteristic of space."

The dozent thinks this far too sophisticated, and reminds the piper of Mujynya's ontological dynamism regarding ntu, each ntu being an active and fragile force.

What would it take to release us from the notion of periodicity? Shall we give in to Hasty, who will tell us that rhythm, as concrete as it might be, has no character?

What do we make of this: "Dialectic is the basis of rhythm, which consequently is more than sheer periodicity, or evenly spaced repetition of any occurrence."

Are we forgetting the edge, that point where the state of the matter abruptly changes? Do we have any sense of continuity? Have we at all understood θέμις, μοῖρα, σωφοσύνη? Do we have any way of expressing sequence without moving within a tensed domain?

This intrinsic architecture we have proposed threatens to involve us in a quarrel with Attridge, and make us susceptible to adopting indefensible fallacies we thought we had overcome.

Should we pay attention here to this? Speaking against any mimetic function for the sounds that occur in verse, Attridge reminds that these sounds "operate normally as constituents of conventional linguistic, or, at most, call up associations with other signs within the system."

Bösendorfer now starts a riff in tune with Attridge, his displeasure with all affective functions. How could the dozent help him to disentangle those rhythms Bösendorfer claims for the act of speaking itself?

Should we return to where we might never have traveled? Should we understand Peirce's index (as Attridge does) to signify something other than itself "not because it resembles that other thing but because it is a direct product of it"?

The piper says we have made the wrong turn. He wants a review of Mujynya's ontological dynamism in four principles. He will deny any Leibnizian monadological imputation, and do not let him start on that *Critique de rythme* that proposes rhythm as "la part la plus archaïque" of any language.

Whose modality can do the work? What have we undertaken to "fix"?

Have we ceased to talk about rhythm? Or have we entered a gate of rhythmic substance, an epistemological lament that responds to unspecifiable laws, to movements that cannot surface, always in transition?

Thalassinos confronts the piper, repudiating his limpid response to the world's transition.

The dozent senses a transcendental calculus in the making, marking a critical opalescence, a "bubbling medium of indeterminacy."

Thalassinos seems prepared to sing the transmutation of his scales, their dissonant modulation and inversion. He knows, without knowing, rhythm's situation.

"Every act arises from a situation. The situation is a constellation of other acts in progress."

Hadn't Mulago instructed Langer to see in the fleet transference of light from body to body a delicate and dynamic ratio?

The dozent thinks that the question has, in this instance, taken the wrong form. This placing rhythm on a plane out of sight of a speech community sings a Kantian bell the dozent does not want to sound.

You must hear Bösendorfer's applause. What, he says, ever hap-
pened to Frege? Ecco, says the dozent, let's hear it for logic.

The piper does not want to count the linguistic turns that seem
to have surfaced without notice and without sanction. Have we
learned that a language "makes it possible *to refer to the same
thing in different ways*"?

Can our piper now entertain those elements of a constructive
design of a dense and complex order that exists in the way that
George Russell says it does—above time?

You will have to notice a certain shadiness in the piper's argument, a willingness to turn through a communicative and a cognitive function of language without specifying either mode.

Remember Aristoxenus

τάξις χρόνων ἀφωριξμένη
Rhythm is an ordering (or a
defined ordering) of time.

Who now wants to continue, given that the piper's dizzying analogy does not want to give up?

"The point is not so much that universal gravitation must be *true*, as that it must be significant—whether true or false is an irrelevant question."

424 SOUL AND SUBSTANCE

Thalassinos always presents himself at the wrong gate. Here now, he talks about a transposition of rhythms, about a transubstantiation of space, about creating a narrative for an absence.

Langer, attentive to any unit of activity, might think that Thalassinos would have to recognize a logical pattern satisfied only by the involvement of a sense of time.

The piper does not like this "sense of time," the gradient sense of all structure that makes for a rhythmic quality. He wants to reestablish boundaries for the shape of a sign that seems to have got lost.

Netz stands apart, keeps his own counsel. Our dozent wants to push a moment of critical opalescence. She asks Netz for a pertinent summary of Hellenistic mathematical style; she reminds him of the fertile trio he has discovered: mosaic composition, narrative surprise and generic experimentation.

Bösendorfer asks for the intervention of other voices. The piper thinks our convocation threatens to misunderstand the significance of our linguistic turn, and the worrisome implication that meaning determines reference.

Does the piper want to insist that rhythm has no meaning? How can the piper handle an epistemology of action and force that cannot find a referent to which it could, if not commit itself, at least propose itself as an event?

Has the piper bound himself into a corner where he has to acknowledge an innermost transmissible motion, or give up the idea of a determinate transformative design?

Trying to keep afloat in an environment turning to deep water, the piper turns to a page from Mudimbe. And there he thinks he might have discovered some sustenance for his wounded propositions in treating with myth.

What can we make of this? "Polysemus, muthos means word and saying, statement and report. Its correspondence with the meaning of fictitious and imaginary story is both a conceptual and semantic extension."

> μῦθός καί λόγοι
> designated legends and truths
> μῦθός / ποιεῖν
> See ⟶ fable / the act of constructing

Do we here, through Mudimbe, make space for conceptual and semantic extension?

Let us ask ourselves now, what is fictitious in mythic activity?
Let us ask ourselves, what is fictitious in rhythmic activity?

Badly formed that. Or perhaps formed too soon, absent any
definition of the field in which the activity occurs.

The dozent sees the piper slowly pressured into looking for an
invariant of surface. She knows our inquiry into rhythm has not,
as yet, turned up a surface of generic experimentation.

We will have to confront this outrage of extension.

428 SOUL AND SUBSTANCE

What are we looking for, without being able to see it? Our choir seems to pay no attention to a notion that keeps surfacing but resisting definition. We speak, the dozent says, of order, and that means number, and the piper doesn't know what to do with that.

The dozent would like to sing with Slaveva-Griffin, looking at her Plotinus, "For Plotinus multiplicity is finite not infinite, and number belongs to the intelligible realm, not to [the] theoretical world of mathematics."

Can we argue that number proper exists separately from mathematical number and that the true nature of number is ontological, not quantitative? Why should this matter?

The piper wants to resist this dozent assault. He resists the idea that number possesses being, and we know it as limited and that it therefore must exist.

Thalassinos wakes up now from his transcendental fog. He urges us to believe that substantial number is substance itself. Our seafarer astonishes the piper with his understanding of the primary properties of substance. Shall we notice them along our way? Being, rest, motion, sameness, otherness.

The piper distrusts Thalassinos's hypothetical insistence. Thalassinos prepares to defend his lessons in Mulago and Mujynya, even though the piper becomes loud about his contradictory being.

Can any substantial number lead us back to a concern with rhythm "in itself," lead us to propose a notion similar to the first axiom in Spinoza's ontology—"Everything which is, is either in itself or in another"?

The dozent has a quarrel with "in itself"; she pretends, too, to stand steadfast against Kagame and those, for her, hard to digest categories that Thalassinos seems to find redemptive.

Should we turn our attention to another conception of space and time, to that Leibnizian "essential distinguishability" that would, as the dozent proposes, flow into the question of rhythm's distinguishability?

The dozent means to fasten us to a notion gleaned from Faraday—a resettling of "invisible lines of force."

The piper holds his head. He sees in the dozent's intransigence a misunderstanding of a category that seems to flag a necessary extension.

We say that Kuntu redeems the categories that Thalassinos has found productive.

> Kuntu = modality,
> relation to other beings

No one will let the piper use his chairmanship of this convocation to compose, among these relations, an argument for disposition, for possession, for an active passion.

Do we think that the piper has given in to an unfounded expression of "all possible relations among all conceivable beings"?

Could Benveniste lead us out of this confusion? He will tell us that "La notion de rythme est fixée." What can we make of this?

πάς ᾽ρυθμος ὡρισμένη τρεῖται κινήσει

translated by Benveniste as

tout rythme se mesure par un mouvement définé

No matter what we say, we seem on the way toward an Egyptian tenor in our discussion.

Do we understand that Hasty has brought the wrong charge against rhythm, telling us that it has no discretion, no self-restraint, no sense of proportion? Bösendorfer feels a wounded pride, having made a prior claim upon that notion, one he says we studiously ignored.

The dozent anyhow wants to go elsewhere, feeling we haven't submitted the piper's gravitation/rhythm analogy to a proper critique. The piper accuses her of paying too much attention to an opposition that treating gravitation as "merely geometry" encourages, thereby ignoring any modified theory of gravitation.

Does this matter? The piper cannot express his chemical roots that go deep into the metric structure of a field he cannot, as yet, specify.

Does rhythm, however we will come to conceive it, rely upon a field that at "every point gives information produced by every 'tone' in the field"?

Nonsense, says Thalassinos. He accuses the piper of forgetting the distinction that promised to open our way. He will now argue that rhythm has no semantic content on its own.

There seems a mistake here. Listen to a Leibnizian report Nach-tomy makes, "As far as the content or essence of an individual is concerned, the concept of the individual is already complete."

The dozent wants to complete the statement. "Yet a concept does not have power to act." Thalassinos does not like the clever way the dozent has escaped a theology, marking this conceptual marking only as possibility.

The piper sees all of this leading to that Egyptian moment where a law of action and the power to act get invested in a phenomenon that does not need them.

The dozent wants to get down to cases. Can we accept rhythm as a complete concept?

Bösendorfer does not like the smell of that. He reminds us that we have not, as yet, given this event a body. He thinks, too, that he might sound an ally in Philippe Sollers, with his appetite for trafficking in numbers and law.

The dozent asks what he can make of this, if we address this "event"?

> je pouvais ressentir sa présence,
> une présence de mots vivants

Or this?

> À cause d'une parole dite dans une autre
> langue accentuée, répétée, chantée—et
> aussitôt oubliée—je savais qu'un
> nouveau récit m'était déclenché.

Bösendorfer wants to stop this song as nothing other than an irrelevant hymn to those who have not reached "un propre rythme."

Do we have here a challenge to that proper récit we have already encountered?

Where have we stopped? Can we not bring our minds to bear on this "event" as Bösendorfer has framed it? We thought, perhaps mistakenly, that we had established an understanding of substance, and, through that, the materiality of this "event," rhythm.

We find ourselves now picking a new quarrel with Leibniz, a quarrel that seems to spin further and further away from a self-sufficient agent that we seem to have designated, rhythm.

Can we accept this special knot, identity defined by Leibniz's law, "two objects are identical (that is, are the very same object) if and only if they share all the same properties, that is, if and only if they are indistinguishable"?

Where have we trapped ourselves? Have we got ourselves into a mathematical bind? Let us call it a reductionist/pragmatist consideration leading to a conception of the limiting case that rhythm, as concept here, will pretend to escape.

Some others will quarrel with those assembled here. Why bother, they will ask, about a scientific adequacy when we enter the domain of "le visage du masque"?

And what can we make of Spinoza's model of logical production, and that stress upon the generative body that seems, to us, on the point of withdrawal?

Should we sound that Spinozistic notion?

> "the . . . nature of a thing is not determined
> and fixed by a purely abstract definition . . .
> a definition is constituted en acte."

We can play here through the many turmoils of Being, treating them all in Leibnizian fashion as a generative or causal definition that entails a principle of construction, a formulation of principle or law of production.

"Air/C'était bien quelque chose d'entièrement inconnu et nouveau qui venait de se prononcer." Something always a part of the place in which it is found.

Shall we return to Plotinus and his substantial number? And how should we understand the

ἐνέργεῖα τῆς ουσίας
the activity of substance?

We got caught following after that "trace that remains withdrawn." Must we now question the notion of rhythm inhabiting a formless domain? Or how should we propose what we must have thought we had established: a domain shaped by an improvisatory shaping of space?

All this under consideration at this moment has surely to lead to dangerous propositions. Ask again, can rhythm withdraw from its own activity?

The question won't take the proper shape.

Meschonnic mocks our understanding of sign. He says we have anyhow entered upon the wrong road. Shall we attend to this?

> *Il n'y a pas d'unité de rythme.*
> Le seule unité serait un discours
> comme inscription d'un sujet.
> Ou le sujet lui-même. Cette unité
> ne peut être que fragmentée, ouverte, indéfinée.

Haven't we learned from the Akan, Manchester, Kubik, Mujynya that no rhythm can be self-fulfilled, or satisfied with any relationship that leads to a single form?

What did we understand when Barbour returned us to Leibniz, and himself asserted, "Space and time in their previous role as the stage of the world are redundant. The world does not *contain* things, it *is* things. These things are Nows that . . . hover in nothing"?

Our dozent contends that we have become much too clever in allowing epistemic access to meanings without referents.

The piper wants to find some way to fit a singular rhythmic analysis that would satisfy the ontological and mathematical distinguishability of rhythm.

What has happened to the intrinsic architecture stressed in improvisatory and innovative fashion, and that depends "on intimate, invisible connections between *here* and *there*"?

Is rhythm the matter of the matter? How can we speak of such passing moments (moments that do not lend themselves to definition) that continue to expand upon their own uncapturable volition?

Why should we ever have thought of removing time from the activity of rhythm? Have we not understood Stengers's fictional being with its indifferently assigned temporal change, counting upon "the depth given to or drawn from an act embodied and subject to unspecified time"?

We have not gone very far in giving Thalassinos's "event" a body. We have to ask again a question that forces us to consider rhythm as an event that turns back upon itself and makes no claims concerning progression of that event we call rhythm.

Shall we slip away from that soul which proposes Logoi as noetic completeness, and avoid all quarrel with immediacy?

Perhaps we should attend to Langer as she addresses a presentational abstraction in art. What should we see, or hear, when she denies that presentational abstraction any technical formula that would carry a pattern from one level of abstractness to another?

We think of the possibility of turning rhythm through the lens of that presentational abstraction, or let us say simply that we might fool ourselves by looking for the notion in a rhythmic analysis.

Listen to Langer: "For purposes of logical analysis, art is unsystematic. It invokes a constant play of formulative, abstractive and projective acts based on a disconcerting variety of principles."

An annoying question surfaces. Can we make a case for rhythm as an imaginative impulse guided by, and in charge of, its own experiential principles?

The dozent wants to put a stop to this speculative nonsense. She reminds us that we have pretended to approve of a prior metaphysical frame, one that almost discounts a body, and sounds that categorematic note we heard before.

Thalassinos might now offer his dissertation on transition, or, stepping over that transitive moment into another realm, transference. He would take this opportunity to question the piper's fundamental assertion of an intrinsic architecture. Nothing predetermined. Only the taking notice of a leap from realm to realm.

Have we arrived at an abruptly closed system, searching for a semantic reality, in which the principal actor has no interest?

Bösendorfer, standing apart, loves to confound us. Consider, he says, Copernicus's commensurability, "all planetary orbits locked into their dimensions by a common measure provided by earth's orbit."

Can our arrangement that we think we seek come to a fulfillment that sounds a transfer of activity, measurable, maneuverable, perhaps ceremonial?

Consider this: "Atoms come and go with scant regard for our sense of unique identity."

Consider this: "Impermanence is not simply a dispiriting fact about the nature of existence, it appears to be an essential part of the reason for existence."

Can we say that rhythms are impermanent? Do they care about their own sense of identity? Can they build from this sense of impermanence an active force? Is action or disappearance of any consequence to the being of any rhythm?

The dozent loves our confusion. She loves the expansive necessity of this suddenly appearing notion of critique, understood as a form of knowledge/self-knowledge.

She reminds us that Gerhard Richter reminds us of Gerichtshof, a court of law for thought itself, and carefully notes the derivation of kritik from κρίνειν (understood as to separate, to choose, to decide).

We must, of course, pay attention to that certain form of post-Kantian critique, which here will establish a self-critique of the principles of reason, and "conceive of critique as a self-constitutive praxis that takes itself as its object in a self-reflexive examination of its own presuppositions and processes."

We have to pause here to find our way back to our rhythm inquiry. What questions now surface? Have we introduced a burden no idea of rhythm will sustain?

Can we ask rhythm for a propositional element? Can we ask rhythm to comment upon itself "as an exclusively self-referential condition of possibility"?

What entanglement now engages us, from the point of view of an "event" that up to now has refused any circumscription that the inquisitive assembly has proposed as a need?

Let us visit a quarrel we probably should avoid. Shall we designate, or at least consider, rhythm as a thing?

We find ourselves confronted by Benjamin: "The true method of making things present to oneself [die Dinge sich gegenwärtig zu machen] is to present them in our space (not to present ourselves in their space)."

What do we make of this? "Learning to practice critique by way of consideration of, and perpetual re-engagement with, thing-world, means learning to read the thing as though it were a text, to be read and reinterpreted again and again, until the real can be read like a text [das Wirkliche wie einen Text lesen]."

"The thing is that which presents the material manifestation of existence to itself as a system of signs to be interpreted by the physiognomist of the world of things."

Whom shall we propose as the physiognomist? How can we account for the author as part of an activity that seems a propositional marker already withdrawn?

How simple can we make any revelatory action? What can we say we look for when we go shopping "semantic content": signs to be interpreted, or things to be rendered into signs?

Listen to this:

choses abstraites (ków) ou des actes wáléw
choses concrètes ou des actes accomplis
(féw ou kí wáléw)

Should we notice here a distinction that seems apparent to the Bamana, and might unravel the idea of movement in a system's interpretation? Can we even discern the various forms of movement suggested here?

Take this as another problem to take to rhythm. The body (let's say, the consciousness of it) must accept a double movement—that expansion and contraction—which might make the signal text unspecifiable.

Notice, please. We keep avoiding time, or we should perhaps say, we find no use for it in interpretation.

Have we dredged up an absurdity here? How do we interpret this?

> Le glā ne désigne pas le vide, fú,
> mais l'étage de la réalisation
> des signes *dans ce vide*, le néant.

What does the piper see for rhythm, having given up time? Or let's propose this as le glā would.

> Le glā décrit le stade intemporel
> et primordial qui a précédé les
> étages de la création.

Does the piper try to sustain rhythm in its self-sufficiency (to speak at the lower level of self-restraint), its ability to remain indiscernible?

The dozent wants no part of this, if we accept rhythm into the world of things. She has already expressed her uneasiness with "in itself."

Let's pretend this thing is alive (still living). The piper might think he has won a point by calling our attention to the terms embodied in "intemporel et primordial."

Shall we treat these as observable properties? We must come to terms with any compound relationship, even though we realize that not all observable properties find themselves gathered at once.

We now pay attention to Munitz, who will give us three conditions necessary for an ens to qualify as existent: (1) being an individual described by application of one or more general terms, (2) being nonfictional, and (3) having a temporal beginning and end.

We look for conceptual bounds by redesigning time. The Duke
would tell us that we do not have to go that far.

But we have caught onto a notion given to us by Munitz: Bound-
less Existence,

        not a proper name, with no object
        or entity to serve as a referent—
        it does not supply an analysis
        of component parts or a list of
        criteria to justify and guide
        its application.

We might ask of this Boundless Existence what we seem to ask
of rhythm. What does it do?

The piper does not run from names, but like Feynman, he pre-
fers to give more of his attention to operations. And our little
gathering seems too inattentive to any set of operations that
would help us to define this ens we call rhythm.

Shall we follow an inquiry into ordered systems, and find here that rhythm, under our gaze, will display a low entropy, with few indistinguishable configurations?

Where would that take us? Our mischievous dozent reminds us that we have given rhythm nothing to defend, and that we have argued it into a freedom that it might not want and might never use.

What a hell of a thing, to come this far with a companion who might refuse your offer of release.

Let us consider bracketing, a notion derived from Munitz. "To bracket is to disregard, disconnect, to suspend normal interests, in order to give heightened attention to what remains and is thereby detached."

Haven't we met this in Pickering's experimenter's theoretical construct?

Yet the chemistry seems confused. Something seems missing from the metabolic processes we have defined for rhythm.

Think on this: "Cells cannot survive without constantly reinventing themselves."

Let's go further into outrage. Shouldn't we consider that rein-vention appears the activity we have denied to rhythm in our inquiry?

We speak of ordered systems. The dozent shows herself capable of reading a paragraph taken from Philip Ball, concerning what she calls a science of process.

Shall we read it with her?

"... chemistry is becoming less about the properties of indi-vidual molecules and more about how groups of different molecules behave together—forging and breaking relation-ships, modifying each other's tendencies, sending out signals."

Can we speak of this ding, this ens, we have been pursuing as an ordered system? To do so we might have to give in to Meschonnic and go from a certain plurality into a manageable singularity. An outrage, perhaps, but, here, a minor outrage.

The dozent wants us to understand the requirements embodied in an intelligent response to an increasingly essential variability.

Can we argue that forging and breaking relationships, modification, obscurity of will and design, might constitute the personality of this ens we have chosen to investigate?

We look for a stability in rhythmic behavior. Perhaps we should reconcile ourselves to a notion similar to what Paul Lockhart and his algebraists express about numbers (a number is what a number does), and pay attention to Rhythmical Reality, observing rhythm engaged in curious and intricate behavior.

Perhaps we need a mass five.

Perhaps we need a mutation that will allow the transmission of a stable pattern.

Unsettling question: Have we arrived at that?

Have we asked the right questions?
We move out of a Boundless Existence into a quantum fix.

Thalassinos does not like the way we have paid little attention to his transitional armory, to the way we have dismissed that "elusively self-referential condition of possibility in living, thinking and acting that never can be reduced to the recording, transmission and reception of a stable meaning."

The dozent might applaud Thalassinos's self-restraint, and Bösendorfer will rise to ask whether we have abandoned our linguistic turn.

Should we now take our inquiry as a post-Kantian legacy marking our critique "as a self-constitutive praxis that takes itself as its object in a self-reflexive examination of its own presuppositions and processes"?

Have we entered a momentarily closed system? Have we turned our Rhythmical Reality into an unapproachable semantic reality in an unapproachable semantic field?

Did we accept an intrinsic architecture and a predetermined inscrutability, relying upon a transference, a leap from realm to realm?

The piper pulses with the notion of his failure; feels that he now must question the mathematical and ontological distinguishability of rhythm; feels that he must give in to rule.

The dozent suggests we return to that Boundless Existence, and do away with an ens proposed "in itself."

We seem now to need to start on a plausible definition of rhythm's field, if not a plausible definition of rhythm "itself."

Do we open another problem: determining a field in movement?

What have we done?
Our little congregation stands astonished by its power.

We have almost made rhythm an orphan, circumscribing its movement, taking away its place in any specifiable movement. Deh! We have taken away its family, and have set about questioning its place and function within that family.

Easy question. One we cannot answer, one that we have allowed to surface and to disappear—un voile absent, surrounded by silence (or let's be exact, by stillness).

What is the question? Have we overlooked the orbital existence of our rhythm?

Given our acceptance of a rhythm orbital existence (if we do accept it), other questions might arise.

Have we overlooked rhythm's distribution in many complex shapes?

Let's visit the dozent's argument against the piper's easy analogy of rhythm and gravity. Any physicist will tell us that gravitation comes "as an effect expected by the metric structure of the field acting locally on any body placed within that field."

We have not, perhaps we cannot, establish a singular field for rhythm, and, along with that, we have not found rhythm's effects upon a field we have not, as yet, established.

At this point, you will note the piper holding his head. He wanted to call upon Leibniz as an ally, encouraged by Munitz who will remind us of what he considers Leibniz's idea of an essential distinguishability—a notion Munitz declares crucial for physics.

How will this notion help our inquiry into rhythm?

And what can we derive from Nachtomy's Leibnizian focus, "The unnatural moment of creating the natural world is, of course, not a moment in time . . . it constitutes time as an order among created individuals. At the same time, this moment of creation also constitutes space as an order among created individuals."

Take this as a plausible summary of our inquiry.

Rhythm →

a transitional figure, whose shape is irrelevant, whose energy is essential, and whose presence is, under certain physical and metaphysical conditions, at times discoverable.

We might find that "visage du masque" a perfect expression of our dance.